Rug Hooking with Fancy Fibers

Sparkle | Shine | Texture

Gail Dufresne

RUG HOOKING

Copyright © 2016 by AMPRY PUBLISHING, LLC

Published by AMPRY PUBLISHING, LLC
Rug Hooking Magazine
3400 Dundee Road, Suite 220
Northbrook, IL 60062
www.amprycp.com

www.rughookingmagazine.com

All rights reserved, including the right to reproduce this book or portions thereof in any form or by any means, electronic or mechanical, including photocopying, recording, or by any information storage and retrieval system, without permission in writing from the publisher. All inquiries should be addressed to *Rug Hooking* Magazine, 3400 Dundee Road, Suite 220, Northbrook, IL 60062

Printed in the United States of America

10 9 8 7 6 5 4 3 2 1

On the front cover: *Gears*, designed and hooked by Gail Dufresne.
On the back cover: *Lizzie*, designed and hooked by Gail Dufresne.
Cover Design by: CW Design Solutions, Inc.
Photography by Cindy Macmillan unless otherwise noted.

Cataloging-in-Publication Data
Library of Congress Control Number: 2016953032

ISBN 9781945550027

Dedication

*This book is dedicated to Maggie McLea,
my first teacher, who without my even knowing it at the time,
put me on the path of most resistance. Thank you, Maggie,
and thanks also to my mother, who brought me
to Maggie in the first place.*

Acknowledgments

Thanks to all of the artists who gave me permission to showcase their work, and who inspire me to keep at it against all odds.

Lydia Brenner
Anne Boissinot
Marilyn Bottjer
Suzanne Conrod
Patti Ann Finch
Linda Gustafson
Jackye Hansen
Nola Heidbreder
Cindy Irwin
Becky Jackson
Tracy Jamar
Lucy Landry
Carla Littlejohn
Cindy Macmillan
Liz Marino
Kris McDermet
Felicia Menin
Gun-Marie Nalsen
Cynthia Norwood
Dick Obernderfer
Constance Old
Barbara O'Connell
Jennifer O'Malley
Chris Preble
Katy Prescott
Sarah Province
Rita Vail
Wanda Wallace
Margaret Wenger
Corinne Watts
Mary Jean Whitelaw
Yvonne Wood

Contents

INTRODUCTION 2

CHAPTER 1
How History Shaped the Art of Rug Hooking 4

CHAPTER 2
It All Started with Maggie McLea 8

CHAPTER 3
Jazz Up the Background 16

CHAPTER 4
Beyond Wool: Introducing Alternate Fibers 28

CHAPTER 5
Add Embellishments 44

CHAPTER 6
Combining Different Needle Arts 48

CHAPTER 7
Combining Rug Making Techniques 65

CHAPTER 8
Looking for Inspiration 92

GALLERY 101

RESOURCES 124

Introduction

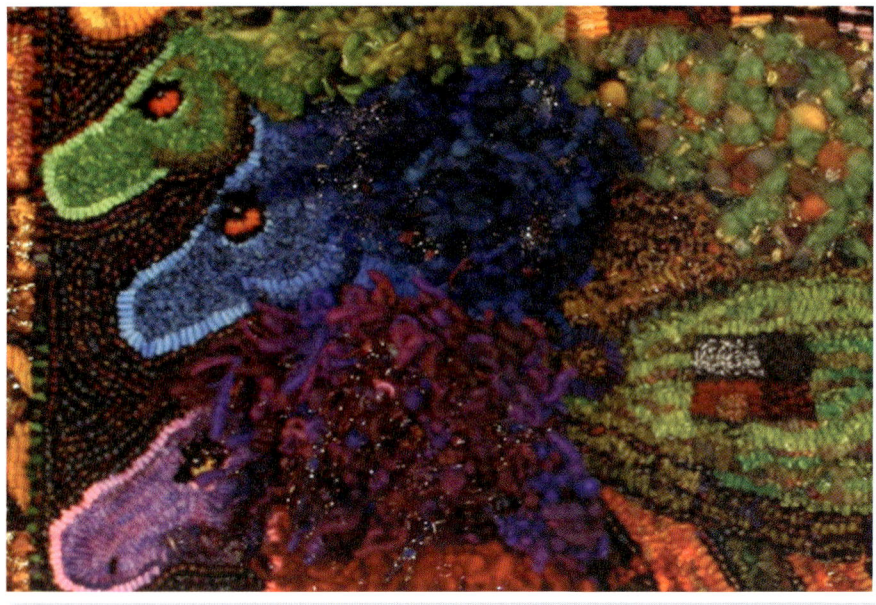

Rug hooking is traditionally considered to be a two-dimensional art form. Don't we measure our rugs by considering only length and width, with no thought or perceived need to consider depth? We even follow a cardinal rule: the loops shall be pulled as high as they are wide. We covet the work of those exceptional technicians who are so adept at this perfect loop pulling. If our loops are not precise enough, we even steam them to make them as flat and even as possible.

But wait! Another world is waiting for you to discover it! You'll be amazed when you see what can be created when a third dimension, depth, is added.

It's What's on Top that Counts

"**Surface design**" refers to any process that gives structure, pattern, or color to fiber and fabric. It's the art of enhancing a surface's structure by applying any number of three-dimensional techniques: weaving, knitting, embroidery, beading, embossing, felting, knotting, netting, looping, stitching, cutting, piecing, quilting, or embellishing.

The purpose of this book is to explore surface design and the infinite possibilities of incorporating different materials and techniques into traditional rug hooking. My goal is to encourage and celebrate boldness, creativity, and the addition of that third dimension of depth. I developed this book for the reader who is interested in learning more about the exciting and innovative work that is being done in the rug hooking world

I included my own work and my students' work, as well as the work of other artists I admire. Some of the pieces stray just a little from what we have come to think of as traditional rug hooking: maybe the artist used a little bit of yarn to fluff up a lion's face, or maybe she blended several wools to jazz up an otherwise flat background. Other pieces employ intricate or unusual techniques and/or materials that are considered cutting edge.

You may have picked up this book to simply read about, enjoy, and appreciate the work of others. Some of the techniques might be beyond your own personal comfort level or current level of expertise.

You may, however, find yourself inspired to experiment just a little. If you have always used one solid wool for your backgrounds, try mixing multiple solids or choosing a texture. Pick a fiber other than wool. Employ a three-dimensional technique such as sculpting or prodding. Take baby steps.

Eventually you may find yourself wanting to go a little further into the mixed media zone and you will know that others have blazed the trail before you. Rug hooking in three dimensions is out there for you to appreciate.

Be Fearless!

When creating art, there are no rights or wrongs.

Using the technique of traditional rug hooking does not mean that you have to actually make a rug. You can create whatever you want for the sheer thrill of it and not worry about where you are going to put the finished piece. There is no need to match a certain room decor or a piece of furniture. You can create just to please yourself. You can follow your own instincts, even if what you are doing is completely different from that being done by everyone around you.

All you really need is a sense of adventure and a desire to play. Don't put undue pressure on yourself by expecting that you will immediately create a masterpiece. Allow yourself time to play for a while. Playing is not frivolous or a waste of your time. Playing leads to discovery and new paths for your creative journey. I, for instance, spent hours making standing wool circles, or quillies, with no thought to what I would do with them, until I had accumulated several jars of them. I now regularly plop them into my work. It was a small step that made a big difference, and I had fun doing it!

Mixed Media Defined

"Mixed media" can be defined as a work of visual art that combines various traditionally distinct visual art mediums. In mixed media, an artist uses more than one medium in a piece of art, such as paint and ink or paint and fiber. The list of combinations is endless, and the number of mixed media techniques used in a particular project is limited only by the artist's imagination and supplies. For many mixed media artists, more is more.

One of the hardest parts about writing this book was deciding how to organize and showcase the work. Many, if not most, of the artists combined several techniques. While it is beyond the scope of this book to explain in detail all of the techniques that were used, I decided to organize the techniques into the following categories, with an example or two under each category.

Experimenting with Different Fibers: Expanding rug hooking beyond wool fabric by using sparkly fabric combined with metallic or other man-made material, silk, velvet, novelty fabrics, or novelty yarns

Embellishing: Adding buttons, beads, seashells, and found objects of all kinds

Combining Different Needle Arts: Using embroidery, beading, weaving, knitting, spool knitting, appliqué, quilting, trapunto, dry needle felting, wet needle felting, or crochet

Combining Different Rug Making Techniques: Sculpting, prodding, punch needle, braiding, standing circles, and shirring

I've also written about experimenting with other fiber arts and artists. Consider the creative challenge called a response mat, a very special collaborative process.

Finally, a gallery, meant to inspire, bedazzle, and enable showcases beautiful, cutting-edge work that combines many of the above techniques.

"To be unafraid of the judgment of others is the greatest freedom."
—Tim Shriver, Chairman of the Special Olympics

CHAPTER 1

How History Shaped the Art of Rug Hooking

Hooked rugs have been called America's one indigenous folk art. Both as a technique and as a means of expression, the practice of hooking materials into a woven base, or foundation as we call it today, was conceived and developed in the United States and Canada, most specifically in Maine, New Hampshire, and the maritime provinces of Canada (New Brunswick, Nova Scotia, and Prince Edward Island).

Exactly when the craft began is debatable, but some evidence dates it to the earliest planting of seeds and agricultural development in the early 1600s. Making do with the minimal amount of materials available to them, women created bed and floor coverings to warm their modest and drafty homes. Both hemp and flax provided homegrown foundations, and natural dyes from barks, berries, and vegetable sources provided color.

These first rugs were workhorses, placed in front of sinks and fireplaces, and they were even used as covers for the woodpile when they were old and worn. Rugs may have been used as casket covers in the northern climates during the winter months when floral arrangements were not available.

The designs at first were primitive, drawn with pointed sticks burned at the tip to create a charcoal tracing pencil for marking on the homespun material. As settlement in the continent increased, so did the art of rug hooking and its complexity.

Geometric designs were made by some of the very first rug makers. Anyone with very basic skills could make a useful floor covering using a homemade foundation, a handmade hook, some worn-out clothing, and a bowl to trace around. Circular motifs were formed by overlapping tracings of a glass or saucer, and ruled, straight lines and square grids could be used for infinite variations.

Even though the first priority in making rugs was utilitarian, its evolution as a means of artistic

Casket Rug, 20" x 36", hemp twine on burlap, traditional rug hooking. Designer, artist, location, and year completed unknown. Photo compliments of Hooked Rug Museum of Nova Scotia.

This casket rug was found in an attic in Canada, stapled to a chair. The image portrays a Bible resting on a tassel cushion. It is surrounded by twigs carried by the dove of peace.

expression began early on. Rug makers sought to put colors together in pleasing combinations and to combine patterns in visually interesting ways. They understood instinctively that the combination of simple basic form and strong color variations could express emotion and rhythmic movement in their rugs.

Images of farm animals, houses, and rural scenes are common, and many include scrolls and floral shapes,

UNNAMED ANTIQUE RUG, 32" x 18" on burlap. Designer, artist, location, and date completed unknown. From the collection of Cynthia Norwood.

This rug maker may have designed her rug by tracing around a cup and a saucer. The negative space (the diamonds) was creatively used and color planned.

UNNAMED ANTIQUE RUG, 52" x 32" on burlap. Designer, artist, location, and date completed unknown. From the collection of Cynthia Norwood.

This rug maker designed her rug with just a straight edge. She then drew the rest of the design free form.

which were often copied from designs on household furniture and pottery. People, ships, and landscapes required more skill and appear less frequently.

In addition to being a domestic activity, rug hooking helped to strengthen community and social ties, for while creating their rugs, women met to exchange ideas and designs. Groups often got together to work on the same rug.

In eighteenth century Europe, in Yorkshire, there was a prosperous weaving industry, but it was expensive to import manufactured goods, which forced Americans to continue to make cloth at home from native raw materials. Any scrap of fiber that was no longer used for clothing was put to good use, often finding its way into a warm rug. It did not matter whether it was wool, and more often than not, it wasn't.

Converting raw wool or flax into cloth was complex and tedious. Textiles were needed for necessities such as clothing, bedding, and linens, and even when used decoratively, textiles were generally considered to be far too valuable to be used on the floor.

Around 1820, samples of jute, an inexpensive natural fiber grown in India, were sent to Dundee, Scotland, which was renowned for its linen production. The Scots perfected the process of weaving jute burlap. The introduction of jute burlap into North America, manufactured for use as feed and grain sacks, made our traditional hooking technique popular and practical. Rug hookers quickly recognized that the loose open weave of burlap and the strength of the jute fibers constituted an ideal base for hooking rugs.

By the 1860s, printed patterns were available, and rug makers no longer needed to create their own designs. By the 1890s, stamped burlap designs appeared in mail order companies such as Sears and Roebuck and Montgomery Ward. The John E. Garrett rug pattern company, based in Nova Scotia, printed and distributed patterns from 1892 to 1974. At the height of its popularity, the company had 20,000 names on its mailing list.

Kris McDermet's ***Tablerunner*** masterfully illustrates a combination of different rug making techniques and different fibers.

In the late 1800s, American manufacturers were producing machine-made rugs for purchase. These rugs were considered superior and of a higher value than handmade rugs, which at this time were associated with poverty and traditionalism rather than innovation and refinement.

A resurgence of handmade rugs occurred in the first part of the 1900s, due in part to the Arts and Crafts movement, which renewed interest in handcrafted work overall, and the Great Depression, which made thriftiness once again more of a necessity.

Also around this time, printed material appeared that specifically encouraged the combination of hand work techniques, especially in borders. In the book *Combining Rug Hooking & Braiding,* the authors write: "For early American women, trained since childhood in the essential skills of needlework, it was easy to combine crafts to create fancier items. They created crocheted collars with beaded edgings, crazy quilts that not only combined scraps of fabric but also showed off exquisite embroidery, and appliquéd pillows with lacework borders. A needlepoint purse might have had a knotted or beaded fringe or an embroidered pincushion might have had a ruffled edge."

Although handmade rugs continued to be made in the second half of the 1900s, techniques were combined less often. As more women started to work outside the home, and as inexpensive imports became more widely available, fewer rugs were made by hand.

In the early 1980s, the Dorr Mill Store, one of the premier wool manufacturers and distributors in the United States, was divided into two sections: one for sewing supplies and another for rug hooking supplies. The store provided an ample supply of Pendleton plaids, tweeds, and checks on the sewing side, but none was available on the hooking side because most people simply were not hooking with textured wools.

Pearl McGown, an incredibly successful business woman who started a mail order pattern business in the 1930s, was convinced that supplying the demand for qualified instructors to teach rug hooking was the key to keeping rug hooking vital. She established herself as a teacher of teachers, and in 1951, she created the McGown Teacher Training Workshops.

In the 1960s, in order to ensure that her teachers and their students had an ample and consistent supply of the wool, Pearl worked with George Dorr (Terry's father) to produce a line of solid wools that could be cut in a #3 strip without raveling. She also gave precise color specifications. Each wool was given a number and could be ordered by that number.

In 1981, Terry attended the first session of the Green Mountain Rug School in Vermont, which was co-founded by Ann Ashworth and Jean Armstrong.

He noticed that attendees were using textured wool in their work. His response was to design four textures that were well suited to overdyeing.

The "rug hooking–weight" line of solid wools designed by Pearl McGown and these four textures can still be ordered today.

It wasn't until 1999 that Rebecca Erb, owner of the The Wool Studio, began designing wool specially milled for the hooking industry.

Today, rugs for the floor can be easily and economically purchased, but the practice of rug hooking is still very much alive. The difference is that now artists choose to pursue the art form rather than having to do so out of necessity. The emphasis is more often on creativity, not practicality. Many trailblazers are exploring exciting approaches to the medium and, in doing so, are broadening the perception and expanding the boundaries of hooked fiber art today.

Their work is redefining the art form through the use of vibrant color and unusual, alternative materials such as paper, plastic, linen, cotton, silk, velvet, wood, and beads. They are incorporating different fiber arts, such as embroidery, beading, felting, knitting, and quilting, and they are incorporating other rug making techniques such as prodding, shirring, and standing wool circles.

A Dorr Mill color card shows the range of colors in rug hooking–weight wools that are available. The four textures at the top left were those Terry designed after attending the Green Mountain Rug School.

How History Shaped the Art of Rug Hooking | 7

CHAPTER 2

It All Started with Maggie McLea

There are many ways to discover the magical world of rug hooking. You may come across a rug display or demonstration at a county fair. Maybe you caught a craft segment on HGTV or The Martha Stewart Show (yes, rug hooking was featured on Martha's show!). Perhaps you found an old rug at an antique show or flea market, or in your grandmother's attic, which prompted you to seek out a book or a group that could tell you more about how it was made.

Rug hooking is a subculture that flies just under the radar of most people's lives, but once you discover it, you find a tight-knit group of people immersed in and bound together by a common interest.

I was lucky enough to grow up surrounded by rugs and rug makers and when I was ready, there were many who were more than happy to help and inspire me. Once I dove in, I never looked back. I wanted to absorb as much as I could and to see where this art form could take me. Nothing takes the place of working with, and being inspired by, fibers and fiber artists.

My first teacher was Maggie McLea, an incredibly gifted artist who was way ahead of her time. Maggie is often remembered as the Queen of Embellishments. She instilled in me a love of enhancing rug hooking with other art techniques. My mother (Doris LaPlante) and my sister (Yvonne Wood) began rug hooking 20 years before me, when I was 14. They took an adult education class in Manchester, Connecticut, with Maggie. When I expressed interest in what they were doing, my mother turned me over to Maggie, who by then had regular Saturday classes at the Fraser Studio in Manchester. People drove from several states away to attend.

Maggie later taught classes every Wednesday at my mother's house for as long as I can remember. She stayed for dinner every Wednesday night, and one of us drove her home afterward. She was part of the family.

Maggie started hooking rugs in 1951. In 1960, she began to study embroidery. She soon joined the Embroiderer's Guild of America and became a needlework teacher. She taught many embroidery and rug hooking classes in the Hartford, Connecticut, area.

Over time, she started to see rug hooking differently. "I began to think of a piece in terms of embroidery in the small or detailed part of the design and then adding hooking for texture."

Maggie used the most unconventional colors and materials that she could find. "I look at a piece and it speaks to me," she said. But rather than just seeing the piece hooked, she also saw needlework, applique, and beads. This vision gave birth to her mixed media experimentation.

Maggie defined mixed media as "using various materials and techniques in a work of art to achieve another dimension and deeper expression." She freely used several cuts of wool in her rugs when no one else did, and she encouraged her students to do the same. She appliquéd an area for a smooth effect or used an Italian form of quilting, called *trapunto*, to apply a piece of spot-dyed wool that might look just like the leaf on her design.

Maggie's favorite type of rug was a pictorial, in which she worked to express certain moods or feelings. She would often apply a real beaded necklace to one of her hooked figures or attach a real little basket with flowers in it. She applied French knots liberally.

Maggie lived in Needles, California, for several years and loved the desert, which she called "anything but drab, dull, or dreary." Much of her work and that of her students reflects that period.

Maggie felt that she was misunderstood because of her unusual hooking techniques and that she "seemed to be ahead of her times." This is truly an understatement! I have never met anyone like Maggie in my 30 years of rug hooking.

Ace of Hearts, 18" x 28", #3-to 8-cut wool and various yarns on linen; traditional rug hooking and sculpting. Designed and hooked by Gail Dufresne, Lambertville, New Jersey, 2003.

Learn the rules like a pro so you can break them like an artist.

—Pablo Picasso

Teaching to Empower Creativity

Maggie's teaching style would most definitely be called free! She had no rules for us, and my sister and I and the rest of her students were using textures and embellishing our designs like no one else we knew back in the 1980s. Maggie readily suggested yarn and other alternative materials, and sometimes even embroidery stitches rather than hooking, to treat a design element. I was familiar with and comfortable using materials other than wool and combining different fiber art forms from the very start. It has always been natural to me to work this way. I don't remember her ever telling me that anything I did was wrong.

In 1996, after several years of having Maggie as my teacher, she, my sister, and I signed up for the McGown teacher training program. I absolutely loved my teachers' workshops, and what I learned there from dedicated and talented teachers. But what a revelation it was! So many rules!

I was told that I should be able to hook in all four directions. I hook in only one direction, because that is the way I hook best, and it works for me because I use a hoop so I can freely twirl the work around as needed. Maggie never told me that I needed to hook in any direction other than the one that worked best for me.

I was told that there is a right and a wrong side of wool. Maggie never told any of us that there was a right side to our wool! We used the side that gave us the effect that we were looking for.

I was told that the only place to start hooking a design was in the middle. Maggie told us that when beginning a new piece, always start with the part of the design that we can visualize in full color and texture. That made absolute sense to me, and it is what I tell my students today. That part of a design that you can visualize from the start is most likely what excites you about your project and how you came to select or create it. I have never had a technical problem that was caused by not starting in the center of my work. I start where the design tells me to start, where it speaks to me.

I was told that I should never ever use dead black or white in my work. Maggie's opinion was to "never use dead white or black, except when necessary." Black and white in combination, when used effectively, produces a bold punch that does not detract from or compete with the rest of the piece, such in my rug, *Ace of Hearts*, where I used black and white to bring the viewer right into the center of the design.

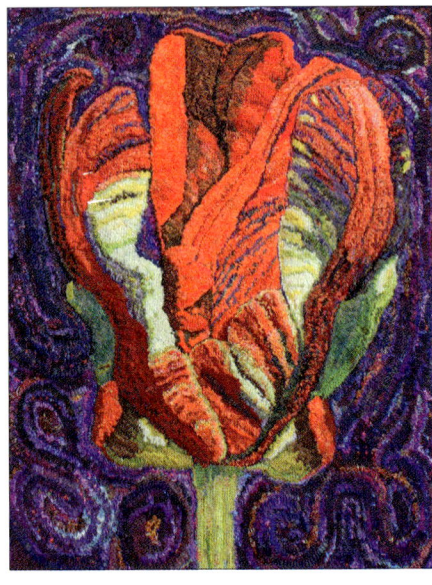

Painted Tulip without the additional borders.

A border of black and white is especially effective in giving a design a defined stopping place. I hooked my rug, *Painted Tulip*, to teach my Wednesday students how to hook as though they were painting. I thought it looked fine without a border, but as an experiment and to demonstrate how borders can change a rug, I worked up a simple geometric border using rectangles of black, white, and colors from the inside of the design. What a difference! I could not believe how much the border enhanced the piece! It contained and completed the design.

I often use a technique called beading, which is holding two pieces of wool in contrasting colors at the same time and pulling up alternating loops of the wool. Most of my work has at least some beading somewhere. I outlined the heart in *Ace of Hearts* with one row of black and white beading. You'll also notice a line of black and white beading, called a "beauty line," between the background and the border of the tulip in *Painted Tulip*. This technique is an extremely effective way to capture the viewer's eye, especially when it's done in black and white wool.

Look outside the rug hooking world to see how many artists successfully use black and white in their work. One of my very favorite artists is quilter Yvonne

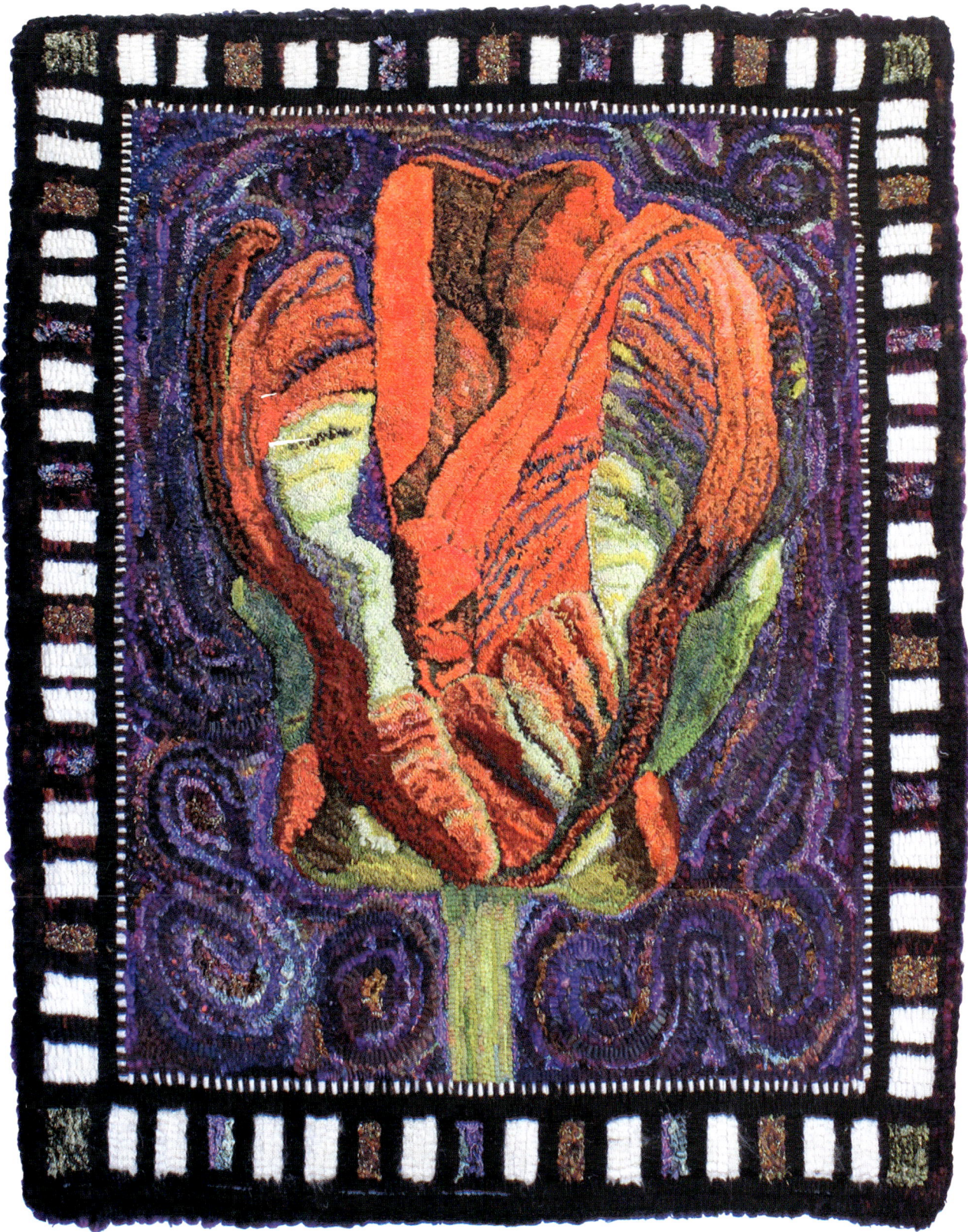

Painted Tulip, 31" x 26", #3-cut wool and various yarns on linen; traditional rug hooking and sculpting. Designed and hooked by Gail Dufresne, Lambertville, New Jersey, 2010.

I designed *Painted Tulip* to be a group project for some of my "home" students. It was not my original intention to sculpt the entire tulip, but it just naturally seemed the thing to do, petal by petal and fold by fold. Tulips aren't flat, so why should my interpretation be flat?

Cactus Wren, 11" x 8", #3-cut hand-dyed wool backing, wool, embroidery floss, and wood scraps, on hand-dyed hookable wool; traditional rug hooking combined with trapunto and various embroidery stitches. Designed by Maggie McLea. Hooked by Liz Marino, South Egremont, Massachusetts, 1999. JANE MCWHORTER

Cactus Wren was designed by Maggie for Liz Marino, another of Maggie's longtime students. Maggie loved to hook through overdyed wool backing, and with her encouragement, Liz employed many embroidery stitches, including French knots. She embellished her work with scraps of wood from her yard.

Porcella, who uses black and white liberally in most, if not all, of her work.

Pretty much everything I believe today started with Maggie. She allowed me to be who I am and to grow into the fiber artist I am today. Right from the start I was encouraged to think for myself and not be held back or intimidated by rules that merely serve to repress creativity, experimentation, and free thinking. Maggie died in 2005, but her influence is undeniable as I incorporate techniques that she taught me decades ago.

One of Maggie's desert scenes called *Southwest Desert* is included in Linda Coughlin's book, *Contemporary Hooked Rugs, Themes and Memories*. This piece was part of a Celebration rug challenge, co-curated by Marilyn Bottjer and Kei Koyayashi.

Maggie's Influence in My Early Rugs

Unlike many rug hooking groups, ours had access to all sorts of textured wool at Jeanette Szatkowski's studio in Manchester, Connecticut, where Maggie's Saturday classes were held. Jeannette and her husband, Bob, owned what is now the Fraser Rug Company, and she sold both hooking and braiding supplies. Bins of various sizes held scraps of wool that were sold by the pound. In these bins were plaids and tweeds that Maggie would suggest we try.

Howling at the Moon, 11" x 14", #4-cut wool and embroidery floss on wool backing; traditional rug hooking combined with trapunto and embroidery. Designed and hooked by Yvonne Wood, Somers, Connecticut, 1990.

My sister, Yvonne Wood, designed a desert scene that clearly shows Maggie's southwestern influence. She used the stuffing technique of trapunto for the wolf and cactus. The cactus is embellished with a variety of embroidery stitches.

Skater's Village, 31½" x 45", # 3- to 5-cut wool and wool yarn on burlap; traditional rug hooking combined with embroidery. Designed by New Earth Designs. Hooked by Gail Dufresne, Lambertville, New Jersey, 1988.

Skater's Village was one of my very first rugs. I love the look and the effect of the embroidered path that meanders through the village. It brought me so much joy that, even though I started it over 25 years ago, I still remember not wanting the stitching to ever end! I embroidered one of the roofs and the church windows. Using embroidery floss, with its sheen, was the perfect medium to achieve a stained glass effect. I hooked in yarn for the children's hats, scarves, and mittens. I chose bits of a plaid skirt or two from the bins for the ladies' clothes.

Detail of *Skater's Village*

OPPOSITE PAGE: *Friend or Foe,* 31" x 40", # 3- to 8-cut wool and wool yarns and fake fur on burlap. Designed by Patsy Becker. Hooked by Gail Dufresne, Lambertville, New Jersey, 1990.

Detail of *Friend or Foe*

I began to work on Patsy Becker's *Friend or Foe* at the Green Mountain Rug School in the late 1980s or early 1990s with another wonderful, forward-thinking teacher, Joyce Crabtree. It was a big hit, because at that time no other class was working with embellishment. Joyce suggested various yarns for the lion's mane, toes, and tip of his tail. I used roving for the tiger's cheeks and ears. After the workshop, I finished the piece under Maggie's guidance. She suggested hooking fake fur for the monkey. I sewed on a piece of material for his tummy. Look at those crazy eyes!

Working with these special materials and techniques was pure joy. I did not worry about whether the alternative materials I selected would "hold up" on the floor, and I did not wonder where I was going to display my finished piece. I was completely immersed in the creative process and focused on expressing myself any way I liked as I created my own personal art. Maggie gave me the confidence to be bold and daring. I was in her world.

If you already know that you enjoy combining rug hooking with other mediums and techniques, or if you are intrigued and wish to experiment, find yourself a teacher who is open to throwing out the rules and encouraging experimentation. His or her influence will shine through in your work and your growing creativity.

CHAPTER 3

Jazz Up the Background

Backgrounds—sometimes referred to as "negative space" because the background is the empty space around the subject matter of the design—can become vast expanses of uninteresting fabric that are as boring to hook as they are to view. How can a rug hooker escape the black hole of negative space? The answer lies in finding creative solutions to add interest to the rug's background without overpowering the focus of the rug's design. Start with wool, then move to other fibers and techniques.

Mixing Solids for Greater Interest

It was in the 1990s, at Southern McGown Teacher's Workshop, that I learned fine shading—and I loved it. One of my first finely shaded rugs was *Thanksgiving*, a very beautiful, complicated Pearl McGown design. My sister told me that it was going to have to be a very "green" rug with all of those vegetables. The challenge for me was to then find vegetables that existed in the real world that were not green, just to prove her wrong.

I decided on a dark background, and the teacher suggested that I use Dorr Eggplant. Just Dorr Eggplant. For the entire background.

The wool in *Thanksgiving's* background

Back then, even though our rugs usually had a greater percentage of background than subject matter, the background was given the least amount of thought. Most backgrounds were hooked in just one solid color of wool, no matter how expansive the area.

I agree that most of the time we do not want our backgrounds to overpower our motifs, but I revolted against the idea that they have to be a vast sea of one flat color.

I wanted more.

Thanksgiving, 47" x 29", #3-to 6-cut wool on linen. Designed by Pearl McGown.
Hooked by Gail Dufresne, Lambertville, New Jersey, 1997.

I chose a mix of about nine different solid wools that were darker and duller than the main motif (the vegetables). In the mix was a wool that was a little brighter, one that was a little lighter, and one that was a little darker. For added interest, I hooked the middle section of the rug (which, I might add, I hooked last!) in a circular pattern, which to me gives the impression of swirling water. I was pleased with the end result, even though my critics told me that it was too busy. I loved it, and I kept it, and I have rarely, if ever, used just one wool in any background that I have hooked since.

Jazz Up the Background | **17**

Combining Solids and Textures: The Next Step

Detail of *Sunflowers*. The darker wool is the Pendleton plaid, which gives the background depth.

I initially planned the background of *Sunflowers* to be several values of a relatively bright sky-blue wool. As I hooked my background, I realized that the values were too similar to those of the sunflowers. The result was a flat and uninteresting background which did nothing to enhance the design. I needed to make a change.

I soaked the wool and laid it into a pan and then spotted it with plenty of chartreuse and navy dye. I ended up with a nicely mottled wool that broke up the monotony of the sky-blue color. Still I felt that something was missing, so I tried adding an undyed (commonly referred to in our world as an "as is") blue and green plaid Pendleton bathrobe. Although there was blue in the plaid of the bathrobe, it was not the same color of blue as the rest of the background. There was also some navy and green in the plaid. The overall effect was a darker and different area that blended in well enough as to not be too jarring, but gave a depth that the solid wool simply could not pull off. It was perfect!

This was the first time that I had used a texture in my background mix and the result was much more effective. I do not think I ever again used just one solid color of wool in my backgrounds.

Sunflowers, 30" x 54", #3- to 6-cut wool on burlap.
Designed by Jane McGown Flynn. Hooked by Gail Dufresne, Lambertville, New Jersey, 1997.

Interesting Backgrounds Led to Geometrics: Busier Still

I became obsessed with backgrounds, or negative space. Its use is a key element in artistic expression. This fascination led me to my love of geometrics, designs that are overflowing with wonderful and ever-changing spaces to fill with color. Although geometric patterns can easily stand on their own, superimposing another image or images over a geometric background makes for an exciting rug and allows for shifting colorplays in the spaces among and around the main motifs.

I hooked my first geometric in 1996, a Jane McGown Flynn design called *Geometric Pot Pourri,* which I was required to complete in order to earn my McGown teacher's certification. The pattern consisted of 40 blocks, or squares, each measuring 5", and I had a terrible time developing a pleasing and cohesive color scheme. The task of hooking a bunch of seemingly unrelated squares at first seemed beyond tedious.

One day, as I struggled with this rug, I was wearing my favorite lizard T-shirt, brought back from a trip to Belize. I thought it might be fun to spread a lizard diagonally across the rug, which would also hide many of those squares that I did not know what to do with. The result was a rug that many thought would get me into trouble when I presented it at the next teacher's workshop, because back then few students, if any, were changing the designs given them to hook.

From then on, it became a challenge to see how wild my background could be and still enhance, not detract from, my main motifs. I, like my mentor, Maggie, was on the road to always trying to find the most unconventional colors and materials I could.

Geometric Pot Pourri, 45" x 28", #3- to 5-cut wool on burlap. Designed by Jane McGown Flynn. Hooked by Gail Dufresne, Lambertville, New Jersey, 1996.

My finished rug did not get me into trouble, and in fact, it was well received by Jane McGown Flynn, Pearl McGown's granddaughter and designer of *Geometric Pot Pourri.* In a speech addressing the workshop participants, she celebrated my courage and creativity in changing the design and making it my own! I was a bit of a celebrity for the rest of that week.

Jazz Up the Background | 21

Work Small When Experimenting

Proddy Sheep, 19" x 22", #3- to 8-cut, linen, wool, and yarn on linen; traditional rug hooking and prodding. Designed and hooked by Gail Dufresne, Lambertville, New Jersey, 2003.

When I experiment with different materials, I work small. I don't choose a huge design with lots of elements to consider. I usually choose a familiar subject that I have hooked before. This piece was my first attempt at prodding and at hooking a painted sky.

Triptych Sheep, three 8" squares, #3- to 8-cut wool, various yarns, and leather on linen; traditional rug hooking. Designed and hooked by Gail Dufresne, Lambertville, New Jersey, 2002.

I started with an 8"-square canvas, hooked the sheep, and then experimented with different color combinations and all sorts of alternative materials in the background. I used roving, yarns, leather, and yes, even wool.

Ruby Pearl, 16" square, #3- to 8-cut wool and angora goat fluff on linen; traditional rug hooking. Designed and hooked by Gail Dufresne, Lambertville, New Jersey, 2002.

Another of my favorite muses is my goat, Ruby Pearl. Likenesses of him have been superimposed on several different geometric backgrounds.

Mini Ruby, 9" x 7", #3- to 8-cut wool, yarns, leather, and angora goat fluff on linen; traditional rug hooking. Designed and hooked by Gail Dufresne, Lambertville, New Jersey, 2003.

My smaller version of Ruby is hooked in the manner of my triptych sheep, with all sorts of yarns, pink leather, and of course, angora goat fluff.

Rudee, 8" square, #3- to 8-cut wool, various yarns, and gift wrapping ribbon on linen; traditional rug hooking and sculpting. Designed by W. Cushing & Co. Hooked by Gail Dufresne, Lambertville, New Jersey, 2002.

Other subjects I experimented with were two reindeer designs that were sent to me in consecutive years from the W. Cushing Company as freebies for ordering around the holiday. I used Christmas gift wrapping ribbon for many of the embellishments—I guess because I had it out and available at the time!

Rudee Too, 8" square, #3- to 8-cut wool, various yarns, and gift wrapping ribbon on linen; traditional rug hooking and sculpting. Designed by W. Cushing & Co. Hooked by Gail Dufresne, Lambertville, New Jersey, 2002.

I found a wonderful yarn that I use to finish the edges of my smaller pieces. It is multicolored, with little threads that fly off in all directions. As someone who sees herself as "sewing challenged," this yarn provides a very forgiving way for me to finish a rug. I bring my mats with me when I teach or speak to show examples of my work. I find that the first thing many people do is flip them over to look at the back (just like we flip over greeting cards to see the price?), so I back my mats with a nice-looking piece of wool. I cut it to size and then sew it on. To cover the edge between the front and the piece of wool sewn on the back, I sew, not whip, my "messy" yarn onto it. The little threads look very cool and cover the edge of the mat—and it is faster than whipping.

Puff the Penguin, 7" x 16", #3- to 8-cut wool, various yarns, and turquoise leather on linen; traditional rug hooking. Designed and hooked by Gail Dufresne, Lambertville, New Jersey, 2003.

    This penguin is cute, but it is the fancy background that I love. The wonderfully vibrant turquoise was one of two leather miniskirts I bid on and won at an auction at a workshop. Actually, no one bid against me and I had no idea then why I wanted it. Now I wish I had more of that miniskirt!

    Note that rather than whipping, I sewed a messy, "thready" yarn to the edge to create a cool effect.

My purple basket holds an endless supply of purple fibers. Another basket holds my favorite green material at the ready. I have become quite partial to purple and was fascinated to reread Judy Fresk's article about Maggie that quoted her as saying that every rug needs a touch of purple! My mix now includes at least as much novelty yarn as it does wool—and purple wool is always around. I keep this basket on hand near my hooking chair and use it for most of my projects. When it gets low, I simply add more fiber. More recently I have added silk sari, silk yardage, velvet, and manmade materials such as cotton, rayon, and spandex. The process of experimenting and incorporating these materials into my backgrounds has been sheer joy. I find the end result to be so much more interesting than just using wool.

Detail of *Lizzie*

Lizzie, 84" x 64", #3- to 8-cut wool and various yarns on rug warp; traditional rug hooking, beading, and sculpting. Designed and hooked by Gail Dufresne, Lambertville, New Jersey, 2012.

I hooked one of my more recent rugs, *Lizzie*, which measures about 5' by 7', with a varied mix of wool, yarns, and sari silk that I keep in a basket that is about 14" in diameter. I more or less randomly pulled materials from it and filled it back up when it got low.

After I hook my backgrounds, I often use a shimmery 100% nylon yarn called Trendsetter Aura. I hook it in last because it is very thin and this is the only way I can get it to stay put. I think of it as a glaze. It is in most, if not all, of the backgrounds I talked about above. It can best be seen in Lizzie's toenails.

Jazz up the Background | 27

CHAPTER 4

Beyond Wool: Introducing Alternate Fibers

Party Animals, 21" square, #3- to 5-cut wool, metallic yarns, gift wrapping ribbon, sequins, fancy trim, and glitter glue on linen; traditional rug hooking, beading, and sculpting. Designed and hooked by Gail Dufresne, Lambertville, New Jersey, 2000.

Party Animals was part of an American/Japanese exhibit, the theme of which was "Celebrations." I chose to represent New Year's Eve. I used all sorts of metallic yarns, gift wrapping ribbon, sequins, and fancy trim. I glitter glued the saxophone.

Sparkle wool with Lurex

In 2005 I was offered the once-in-a-lifetime opportunity to teach at the Reeth Rug Retreat in England. In England, the cost of wool is so prohibitive that rug hookers rarely use off-the-bolt wool for their projects. It was the first time I saw many students using materials other than wool in their work. Instead, they used recycled wool and cast-off clothing, regardless of fabric content, as well as leftover yarns and non-fabric materials, such as plastic bags. If they can make loops with it, they hook with it. They work much like the first rug makers did, using whatever they have on hand.

English rug hookers often design their own rugs because there are few pattern makers in England and ready-made patterns are expensive. What they create is amazing and exciting, and observing their works in progress freed me up even more to work outside the traditional rug hooking box. It also made me fully commit to designing my own rugs. Yes, there are wonderful designs that can be purchased and adapted, but I began to appreciate the thrill and satisfaction of creating exactly what I wanted. It is a big leap for some of us to make because it is often easier and faster to simply use someone else's design, and we tend to doubt our artistic capabilities, but I knew it was time.

Purple Mixed Mania, 10" x 42", #3- to 8-cut and hand-cut wool, various yarns, velvet, and novelty fabrics on linen; traditional rug hooking, appliqué, trapunto. Designed and hooked by Gail Dufresne, Lambertville, New Jersey, 2009.

  Purple Mixed Mania uses all sorts of material from my purple basket. I sewed materials atop this rug to give it even more dimension and to highlight certain materials I especially loved. I used lots of different pieces of velvet given to me by one of my English students who lived near a velvet factory in England. She had accumulated so much of it that she had a separate storage area on her property to house it all.

Sari Silk

One of my favorite materials to use is silk. Silk gives a sheen that wool cannot. I discovered sari silk, a by-product of the colorful saris manufactured in India. The silk is cut into strips, so it is ready to use. It is available in ribbon or in spun yarns in gorgeous colors, but it can also be purchased in white or off-white, which can be dyed with the same acid dyes we use to dye wool.

Multicolored sari ribbons. The 100% silk sari ribbons are made from the waste ends of silk sari production, which are collected from industry weaving mills in India and sewn together to form a continuous length. Choose from a multicolored ribbon with smooth ends or one with fuzzy ends

Solid color sari ribbons. The solid colors of ribbons have been dyed to one color, but expect a ton of variation in color and texture, including bits of beads and embroidery from the original saris.

Chiffon sari. Also look for skeins of ribbons made from strips of patterned silk chiffon fabric. Many of these strips also have little treasures of sequins and embroidery in them.

Sari yarn. The yarns are made from the same waste ends as the ribbons. The yarn is hand teased and then hand spun on a drop needle.

The ribbon strips vary in width, but can be as wide as 1" or more. A very different look can be achieved depending on how you hook them. Try hooking low, at the same height as the fiber around them, or hook higher than surrounding loops to accentuate a line. You can cut or fold the silk in half for a neater look, or just pull up the loops as they come for a wilder look.

Close up of *Sari Fish* border (full rug on page 34). In *Sari Fish*, I pulled up and manipulated each loop by hand, straightening out the loops to show the detail in the ribbon. The loops are about ¾" to 1" higher than the hooking around it.

One of the very best uses for this ribbon is as a border for a rug that has not been drawn straight on the grain. Simply draw a straight line around the design perimeter and use large loops of sari ribbon to cover the entire uneven edge. Voila! A straight edge to a crooked rug!

Close up of *Gears* border. Sari ribbon makes a very effective border. I like to use the multicolored ribbon strips in the order in which they were sewn together. In *Gears*, I kept my border loops low, about ½" high. See the full rug on page 69.

Silken Galaxy, 24" x 28", #4- and 5-cut wool, beads, sari silk ribbon on linen; traditional rug hooking. Designed and hooked by Sarah Lee Province, Silver Spring, Maryland, 2012. IMPACT XPOZURE

Sarah Province hooked yarns and ribbon higher than the rest of her material to accentuate the elements in her silken galaxy. I would like to visit this beautiful galaxy!

San Antonio Mixed Media Mat, 10" x 14", #8-cut and hand-torn wool, various yarns, and sari silk on linen; traditional rug hooking, prodding, and standing wool circles. Designed and hooked by Gail Dufresne, Lambertville, New Jersey, 2014.

San Antonio Mixed Media Mat is a learning piece to familiarize a beginner with mixed fibers and techniques. Much of it is sari silk. The shimmer of the fuchsia silk ribbon prodded into the border makes it glow.

Beyond Wool: Introducing Alternate Fibers | 33

Sari Fish, 20" x 14", #3- to 8-cut wool, various yarns, and sari silk on linen; traditional rug hooking and sculpting. Designed and hooked by Gail Dufresne, Lambertville, New Jersey, 2013.

Sari Fish incorporates every kind of sari silk I had. The border is hooked with multicolored ribbon. The fish is outlined in lavender pure silk yarn, and within that outline, I outlined it again with purple chiffon. Each section inside the fish is outlined with the same purple chiffon.

Starting at the head of the fish, the lime green, fuchsia, and gold sections are silk chiffon sari. The fuzzy, lighter multicolored sari running the length of the fish just behind its eye is Himalayan soft silk yarn. Just behind that is multicolored thrum yarn.

I used lavender and jade wool, not sari silk, for my background, which I hooked with a #3 cut, sheared, and then re-hooked using Trendsetter Aura yarn.

How to Make a Shiny Bubble

The bubbles are textured wool that was sewn on and stuffed with dryer lint, a technique called trapunto. I then laid an iridescent fabric and stitched over that with silver thread. The bubbles are outlined in the same lavender pure silk yarn as the fish.

34 | *Rug Hooking with Fancy Fibers*

Coordinate Your Fibers: Wool yardage, wool yarn, sari ribbon, Dupioni silk, silk charmeuse, and wool/silk blend dyed together in the same pan.

Dupioni Prodded Sunflowers, 10" x 13", #8-cut and hand-torn wool, various yarns, novelty fabric, sari silk, silk brocade, Dupioni silk, and felted balls on linen; traditional rug hooking, prodding, trapunto, and standing wool circles. Designed and hooked by Gail Dufresne, Lambertville, New Jersey, 2014.

You can see how vibrantly dupioni silk takes the dye. I don't mind a little fraying in the prodded flowers. The frayed bits can be trimmed or treated with a liquid seam sealant.

Silk Yardage

It took me some time to make the leap from using sari silk to using silk yardage. Like wool, silk is a protein fiber and can be dyed using the same acid dyes that are used for wool. That means that you can dye silk, wool yardage, and wool yarn in the same pan. The colors will not look exactly the same on the different fibers, but they will be related. Realizing that I had the capacity to dye silk any color I pleased made the leap to silk yardage easier.

There are many different styles of silk. For example, Dharma Trading company sells over 50 varieties, and for a nominal fee they will send you samples of each. Take advantage of these types of offers, because each style of silk has its own distinct characteristics.

Because silk does not have the "body" that wool has, it is more manageable when cut and hooked in wider strips. I like to cut or tear it into 3/4"- or 1" widths and then fold it into itself.

Silks that I have found to be fairly well suited to pulling up loops include dupioni silk, charmeuse, crepe de chine, and a 63/37 wool/silk blend.

Dupioni Silk

Dupioni has intentional slubs in the fiber, giving it a wonderful texture. It has a crisp, firm hand with lots of linear texture and subtle luster, and it dyes brilliantly. Dupioni silk is stiffer than the other silks I use, and it frays quite a bit, but I love the way that it takes the dye. It will only tear in one direction (perpendicular to the selvedge), so you need to pay attention or you will tear it off the grain. I save Dupioni silk for techniques other than traditional hooking, such as prodding or trapunto, where the fraying can be more easily managed and can be an asset rather than a nuisance.

Charmeuse

Silk charmeuse is a shimmery, soft, drapey fiber that has a luxuriously smooth texture. It is gorgeous to touch and to work with. It does not fray as much as Dupioni silk. It just folds into itself as you loop it, for a wonderful, lush look.

Learn from many different sources. Let the experience and instructions of others filter through you until little particles here and there are caught and merge into something that feels just right for you.

—Mickey Lawler (quilter)

Table Runner, 18" x 39", #5- and #6-cut wool and silk charmeuse on linen; traditional rug hooking and braiding. Designed by Kris McDermet and Lynn Hoeft. Hooked and braided by Kris McDermet, Dummerston, Vermont, 2014.

Artist Kris McDermet, who regularly combines hooking and braiding, loves the shimmer of charmeuse and especially loves the effect of red charmeuse. She combines it with wool strips to braid, stuffing the silk strips to match the thickness of the wool strips.

Crepe de Chine

Crepe de Chine is one of the more luxurious of the silks, and it is available in several weights. The heaviest weight sold by Dharma Trading company is divine. It has a slightly crinkled texture with a gentle, graceful drape, a very soft hand, and is of a more substantial weight than the other silks I use. Because of the texture, the sheen is subtler than that of charmeuse. It does not fray as much as Dupioni silk.

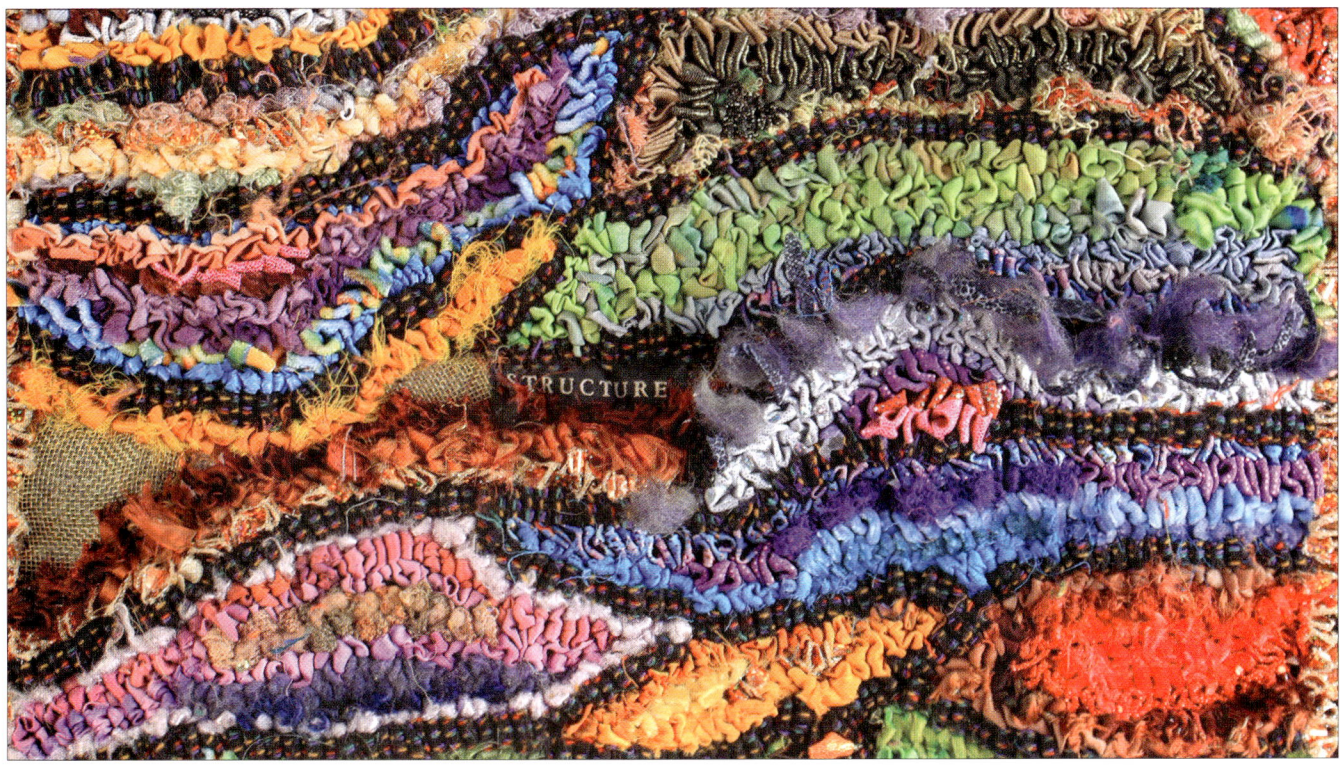

Detail of *Structure*.

Wool/Silk Blend

Dharma also sells a wool/silk blend. Lightweight and semi-sheer, this fabric is softer than wool and does not have the sheen of Dupioni silk or silk charmeuse. However, it is soft, easy to hook, and gives an interesting, gauzy texture.

Silk Brocade

Embossed fabric such as silk brocade is gorgeous but very difficult to hook. Threads, often silver or gold, are added to the main fabric, producing a raised relief. In some brocades, these additions present a distinctive appearance on the back of the material where the supplementary weft, or floating threads, of the brocaded sections hang in loose groups. When cut, it frays and these threads fall away. I could not resist such beautiful fabric when I was shopping at Mood Designer Fabrics (where the lucky contestants on *Project Runway* shop), so I bought it anyway and set to work thinking of ways I could use it.

Silk brocade is great to use for trapunto, as I did in *Dupioni Sunflowers*. Trapunto is a quilting technique that involves stuffing a fabric and sewing it to the rug. The technique highlights the beauty of the fabric.

Beyond Wool: Introducing Alternate Fibers | 37

Velvets made from a variety of materials, including rayon, silk, polyester, nylon, and cotton. Velvets vary in weight, density, and durability. A soft, stretchy velvet made of rayon is easier to work with than a heavy velvet made of cotton, which has no give and has more of a tendency to fray.

Velvet

I have always loved velvet. Who doesn't? It is soft to the touch, smooth, and luxurious. It is easy to work with and probably my very favorite material. The hardest part of using it is cutting it, since it has a tendency to slip. I cut it with the velvet pile down. Like silk, it is so soft it folds into itself, and is easier to use in wider cuts. I prefer a #9 or #10 cut. Velvet hooks up much lighter than it appears when unhooked; the value difference is greater than that between hooked and unhooked wool. Be sure to test it before you commit to it for your piece.

Velvets made entirely from silk have market prices of several hundred dollars per yard. You'll find a very long list of types and weights of velvets, each available in a variety of colors and prints; some are even embossed. I encourage you to do your own research if you truly fall in love with the look and feel of velvet.

I now have a large variety of velvets. Some I bought at designer fabric stores like Mood Fabrics, but it is quite expensive. When I really got into using and marketing it, I wanted to be able to dye it myself, so I found and bought yardage from Dharma Trading Company that is a blend of 18% silk, 82% rayon.

In my first attempt at dyeing velvet, I tried the acid dyes I used to dye wool. The end result yielded a very pale fabric because the velvet that I use is made up of a high percentage of rayon. Rayon is not a protein fiber and therefore cannot be dyed with acid dyes. I did not want to invest in another type of dye, so I tried my old W. Cushing & Company all-purpose union dyes. These were the dyes produced by the Cushing Company before they reformulated them as acid dyes. They work beautifully. So now when I dye this velvet blend, I use a combination of my newer acid dyes and Cushing Union dyes to ensure that both materials are properly dyed and to get the level of saturation that I want.

Detail of **The Candy Store**. I was first introduced to hooking with velvet in 2005 when I taught in England. One of my students shared some of her velvet with me, and it is one of the materials in my stash that I treasure most. I used most of the colors she shared with me in *The Candy Store*.

I found a second wonderful velvet at Dharma, which is a stretch silk velvet, a blend of 82% rayon, 9% silk, and 9% polyester. It stretches widthwise and on the bias, but not lengthwise. It does not slip, or "walk," like other velvets that have less stretch, making it easier to run through the cutter with little to no fraying.

Pink Prodded Velvet Flower, 5" diameter, hand-torn velvet, including embossed velvet, Dupioni silk, and sari silk on linen; traditional rug hooking, prodding, and trapunto. Designed and hooked by Gail Dufresne, Lambertville, New Jersey, 2014.

This *Prodded Velvet Flower* was fun to make. The piece of material in the foreground is embossed velvet. The center is Dupioni silk stuffed and sewn on in trapunto fashion, circled with sari silk.

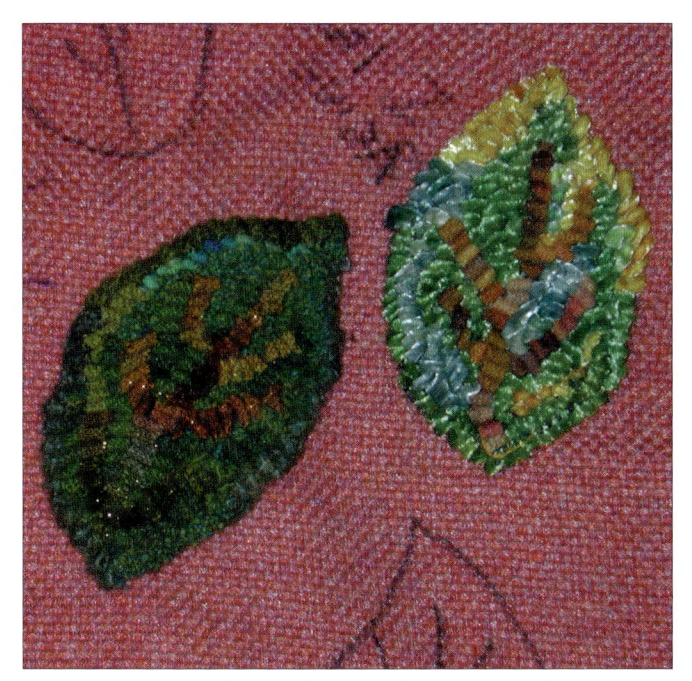

A good example of the difference in the look of wool and velvet can be seen in these two leaves. The leaf on the right was hooked with velvet.

This leaf was part of a challege. I used wool, charmeuse, sari silk, crepe de Chine, velvet novelty fabric, and bouclé. I finished the edge with my messy yarn.

Other Favorite Hooking Materials

Some of my favorite wools, mirror yarn, and fabric. In addition to silk and velvet, I have a stash of "go to" material that I use over and over again in my work.

Some of my favorite yarn. When I see a yarn I think might be suitable for rug hooking, I buy it in every color I can. As trends in knitting change, so does the availability of certain yarns, so I grab what I want for rug hooking when I find it.

The Sun is Always Shining, 27" x 18", #9-cut wool, sparkle Lurex wool, eyelash yarn, and sparkle novelty fabric on linen; traditional rug hooking and crochet. Designed and hooked by Nola Heidbreder, St. Louis, Missouri, 2012.

Nola Heidbreder and I share a love of a fabulous novelty fabric that is made up of little mirrors. I own yards of it in many colors and use some version of it in much of my work. In *The Sun Is Always Shining*, Nola, who likes to hook her granddaughter and herself as chickens, used mirror fabric, or what she aptly calls "ruby red slipper fabric," for Hadley's bathing suit.

Cotton

A quilter gave me a big box of beautiful cotton strips in all sorts of gorgeous colors and patterns, but I did not start to use them until I saw another quilter was liberally using cotton in her work. I loved the distinct shine and the varied patterns. The loops do not fluff up as well as wool, but the colors are vibrant and the sheen differs from anything else. I now liberally add cotton into in my mixes.

Material that has a bit of stretch, like wool, is easier to hook. Cotton, for instance, and materials made with cotton, such as denim or velveteen, do not give like wool. The same is true for leather and Ultrasuede—but that doesn't mean you can't use them.

Spandex is my most recent addition to the mix.

Spandex

Spandex, now often called Lycra, was invented in 1958. It is a lightweight synthetic fiber used to make stretchable clothing: think bathing suits, yoga pants, and the life-changing addition of it to our jeans. (Remember when jeans had no give?) Spandex is exceptionally stretchy, strong, and durable.

I use my cutter to cut Spandex. You may not want to do that, but my philosophy is that I get the best cut by using my cutter and I will buy a new blade when I need to. Nothing reacts quite like Spandex! It has a mind of its own. It can be cut in small cuts but I like to use wider cuts so that you can see the pattern and the shine. It pulls up more like cotton than wool, as it does not have the fluffy texture of wool. The ends are very blunt and sometimes white and rubbery looking, so I do not pull them up—I leave them down.

Red Velvet Poinsettia, 9" diameter, hand-torn velvet, Dupioni silk, and sari silk Spandex on linen; traditional rug hooking, prodding, and trapunto. Designed and hooked by Gail Dufresne, Lambertville, New Jersey, 2014.

I used several different colors of Spandex in the background of this prodded poinsettia. One of the Spandex pieces is the shiny purple with polka dots.

Working with Unusual Materials

Lurex is the registered brand name for a type of yarn with a metallic appearance. The yarn is made from synthetic film onto which a metallic aluminum, silver, or gold layer has been vaporized. Here, Lurex has been woven into wool yardage to give extra shimmer to fabric.

To Cutter or Not To Cutter

I am often asked if cutters should be used to cut material other than 100% wool. In 2004, I wrote an article for *Rug Hooking* magazine comparing the different cutters on the market at that time. They were the Bliss, the Fraser-500 (both from the Harry M. Fraser Company), the Rigby, The Townsend (now the Bee Line-Townsend), the Honey Doo, and the Bolivar.

A crucial difference is in the way these machines cut material.

The two Fraser cutters and the Rigby cutter employ a crushing action to cut fabric. The cutting heads are beveled and pressed against a flat pressure roller. The heads will probably need to be sharpened or replaced at some point. The crushing action can allow the blades to become covered with soft materials, such as plastic, and to become chipped by hard materials, such as metals.

The Honey Doo, Bolivar, and Bee Line-Townsend cutter blades are made from hardened steel and cut with a scissorlike action rather than a crushing action. The wool is pulled between opposing rollers and cut by the shearing action of the blades. Because of this they never require sharpening and should not be harmed by cutting any material except for one with a fairly high metallic content.

I have used my Bee Line-Townsend cutters and my Bolivar cutters for many years, and I have cut hundreds of yards of material with them both. My students have used them as well. I regularly cut wool with Lurex as well as materials such as silk, velvet, brocade, leather, Ultrasuede, and Spandex. After all of these years, my cutters are cutting fine and I have not replaced a single blade.

In any event, I consider my cutter to be a tool. Springing for a new blade every few years is not unreasonable. Nothing lasts forever. When my blade dulls or no longer cuts properly, I will buy a new blade.

According to Caryn Devlin (designer with her husband and user of the Honey Doo cutter) the Honey Doo can be damaged by trying to cut wool that is too thick. If the materials you choose are very heavy, therefore, such as coat-weight wool or heavy blankets, I suggest using either the Fraser 500-1, the Bliss, or the Rigby, since they have adjustable tension bars and can handle thicker materials. You can also try a rotary cutter.

Steaming Novelty Materials and Three-Dimensional Work

Be careful when using "mystery materials," those of unknown composition, that may have a lower melting point than wool. Nylon and silk can take at least as much heat as wool can, but polyester cannot.

If you have worked diligently to create a three-dimensional piece, there is no need to steam the part of the work that is raised. If you find steaming around the intentionally raised areas necessary, carefully steam around them.

Storage

Storage was certainly less complicated when I just had to deal with wool! The urge to experiment with different materials and embellishments makes throwing anything out next to impossible. I use containers that are see-through, such as the plastic bags blankets come in. I use lots of baskets. I have an entire closet of yarns stored in wire bins.

5
CHAPTER

Add Embellishments

Cat House, 32½" x 28", #6-cut wool and a variety of embellishments on linen; traditional rug hooking. Designed and hooked by Jennifer O'Malley, Telford, Pennsylvania, 2011.

Embellishments are any kind of ornamentation added to provide dimension, height, and visual interest to your work. You are limited only by your imagination as to what you choose to use to embellish: buttons, buckles, sequins, zippers, shells, semi-precious stones, the occasional lone earring, sentimental trinkets, and beads are just the tip of the iceberg. Any of these embellishments can be added while you are working on your piece or as a final step. They can be used to call attention to features you wish to highlight or to disguise features you wish to hide (like a seam).

Jennifer O'Malley initially created a design specifically to house her extensive cat pin collection. That original idea snowballed into a really fun rug that is now home to many meaningful mementos from her family and friends. The story came together as she studied her collection of pins. The cats needed a house to live in. A clockworks pin inspired the grandfather clock, so she created the house in dollhouse view, so that the viewer could peek inside. She used her grandfather's watch fob as the outdoor light on the left side of the house, so it only made sense to have a night sky. Her son's Statue of Liberty key chain located the house in New York City overlooking the Hudson River. Her mother-in-law donated her Avon award pins: the door knocker, little telephone on the table, and the shooting stars over Lady Liberty. Many of the donated items came from onlookers as she worked on her rug. What a great challenge of the imagination to design the entire piece around the embellishments in front of her!

Many embellishments (the beads in the bushes, the windows on the buildings, the star buttons, the birdhouse, the birds, the phone, and the clock) were sewn on using all-purpose thread pulled tight below the loops to hide as best she could. The cat pins were pinned on using the built-in clasps. Some stick pins (the cat in the top window, the shooting stars, and the black cat at the step) had a round back spring clasp. She pushed the pin through the backing, used a small piece of duct tape to secure it, and then hot glued it. She left the background unhooked for the embellishments she would add on in the end.

Embellishments | 45

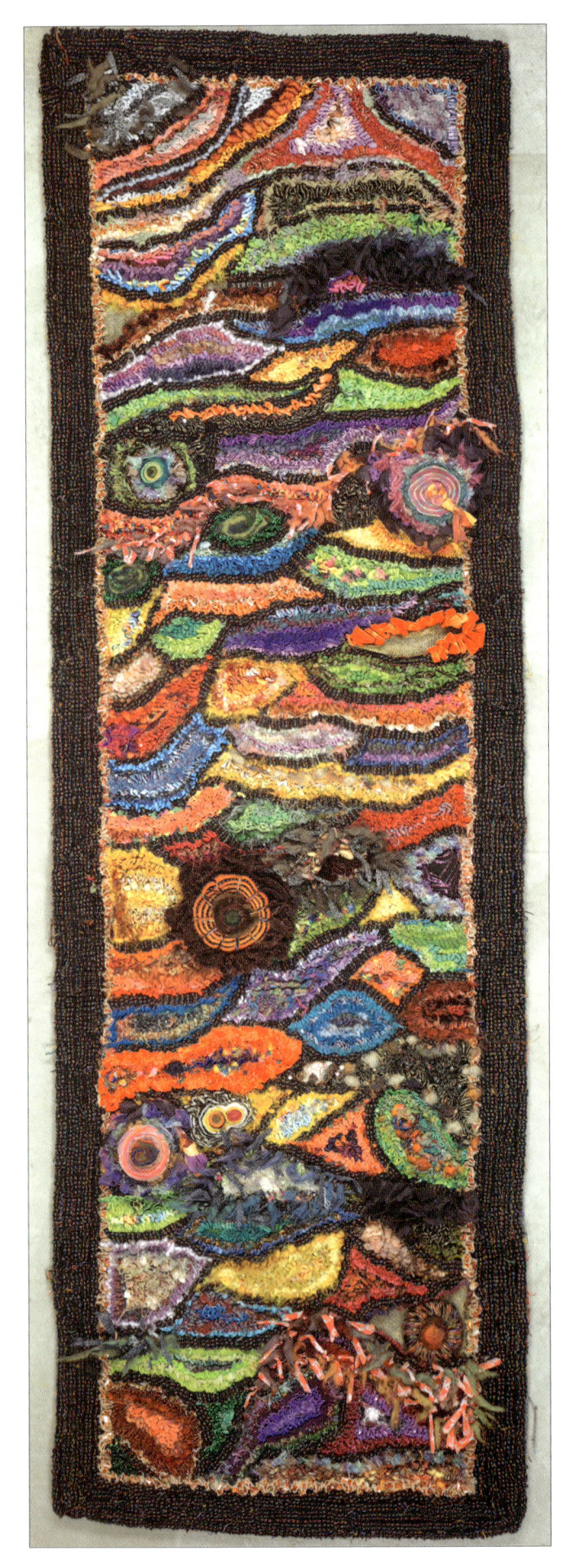

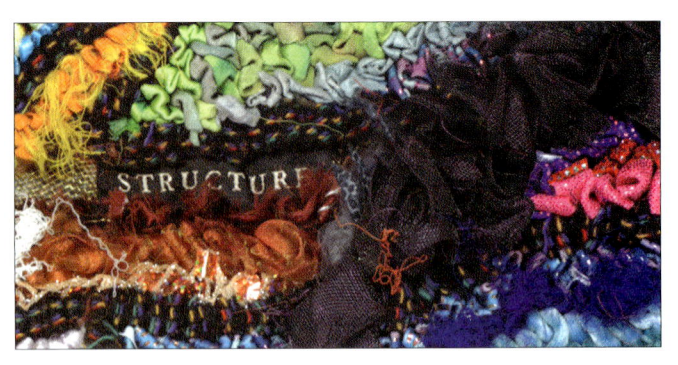

Structure, 21" x 60", various cuts of wool, silk, sari silk, silk ties, novelty fabric, novelty yarns, plastic bags, toilet paper wrappers, used laundry sheets, organza, copper netting, tie labels, and gym mat grommets on Verel; traditional rug hooking, prodding, trapunto. Designed and hooked by Gail Dufresne, Lambertville, New Jersey, 2015. IMPACT XPOZURES

While researching different fibers and embellishments, I began a new project on a piece of Verel, a polyester backing, and planned to hook or apply all sorts of materials as I discovered them. I used my favorite black textured wool for the border and wavy grid lines. I used all sorts of materials on this piece, including wool, sparkle wool with Lurex, silk, silk sari, silk ties, novelty fabric, novelty yarns, plastic bags, toilet paper wrappers, Spandex, color catchers (used in the washer to keep colors from running into clothing), organza, copper netting, tie labels and gym mat grommets. I kept going until I reached the end of the length of the Verel—the final rug was 5' long.

The label on one of the ties that I hooked with was "Structure." I decided that was a great name for this piece. I sewed the label on with waxed thread, which is strong, long lasting, and waterproof. I sewed a bit of copper wire over the label and other areas of the unhooked backing, also using waxed thread. I attached the gym mat grommet onto an unhooked area and to hide the waxed thread I resewed over the grommet using a yarn I liked. Before I knew it, the grommet was no longer visible!

Once I found waxed thread I bought it in every color and use it for everything. It is a staple in my studio. Glue or no glue? It is a personal preference. I try to stay away from it, but if nothing else works and I must use glue, I use E6000 permanent craft adhesive, which forms a powerful bond with almost any material and will remain flexible once cured. It is industrial strength and can bond wood, fabric, leather, ceramic, glass, metal, and more. It remains flexible, even in extreme temperature conditions and is waterproof. It can even be painted once it is cured. When using embellishments, you need to consider not only how to attach them but when to attach them. I use a hoop, not a frame, when I hook, and it is very difficult to get my hoop on over embellishments, so I try to plan beforehand where the embellishments will go and then attach them at the end when the hooking is complete. While still hooking, I place them where I want them and take a photograph so I remember what my plan was.

Mike's Career Rug, 40½" x 30½", #8-cut wool and a variety of embellishments on linen; traditional rug hooking. Designed and hooked by Jennifer O'Malley, Telford, Pennsylvania, 2012.

Jen's second embellished design celebrates her husband Mike's career in corrections, law enforcement, and private investigation training. It highlights his badges, mementos, and awards. The placement of the elements followed Mike's career path, starting at the bottom left and zigzagging up to the top left. A funny story that accompanied each career was illustrated, such as when a duck got into the patrol car, or when a stolen lawn sheep was found in the front yard of the Towamencin Police Department.

The shirt patches were sewn on with all-purpose thread in matching colors. Jen attached the ID badges by piercing them with a fat needle in each corner. The metal badges were pinned to unhooked areas of the backing. Like her cat stickpins in her *Cat House* design, all of the stickpins in the upper left and on the Towamencin Police Station were secured with hot glue. The training billboard items in the upper left corner that were removed from embroidered training shirts were stretched and glued over foam board and then attached to the backing after first sewing fabric to the backing. Then she hooked around them to get the edge to the same height. Many items were sewn on with all-purpose thread.

Embellishments | 47

CHAPTER 6

Combining Different Needle Arts

Many artists are combining different needle arts in their hooked pieces. Consider the possibilities of embroidery, beading, weaving, knitting, spool knitting, appliqué, quilting, trapunto, dry needle felting, wet needle felting, and crochet. In this chapter, I've collected examples of each.

The original appliqué piece, the inspiration for *Mother's Day, 1964*.

Embroidery

After her mother passed away, Lydia Brenner found the little cloth appliqué piece she had made in Montessori school in Holland for Mother's Day, 1964. Her mother kept it in a drawer, carefully preserved. Lydia also found a necklace she had given to her mother when she was a little girl. She knew that she would never wear it, but she couldn't bring herself to throw it away. She decided to combine the two mementos into a hooked piece. I drew the design for her on linen, and we selected wool that gave the feel of the little cloth pieces in her original appliqué.

The medallion of the necklace became the flower. She found a red button from her mother's belongings that fit in perfectly and used a clay tile to recreate the fabric with the chickens that she didn't like—but I

Mother's Day, 1964, 14½" x 17¼", #6-cut wool, yarn, embroidery floss, sari silk yarn, soutache cord, clay tile, clay pocket heart, and necklace medallion on linen; traditional rug hooking and embroidery.
Designed and hooked by Lydia Brenner, Fair Haven, New Jersey, 2013.

loved. She embroidered the Dutch word for Mother's Day with embroidery floss. The finishing touch was the clay pocket heart given to her by Lisa Luckett, who passes out the hearts to friends and strangers who cross her path. Lydia immediately knew that the heart belonged on the rug.

She whipped the edge of her piece with sari silk yarn. Hooking the little rug allowed Lydia to peacefully work through her mother's death and reflect on their relationship.

Combining Different Needle Arts

Couching

Couching is an easy-to-learn embroidery technique, which creates a striking and effective embellishment. Anne Boissinot pins cording loosely onto her backing and bastes it into place. She then whips it over and over with her material of choice to cover the cording.

Anne used a multicolor dip-dyed yarn to whip over the cording that she basted in place.

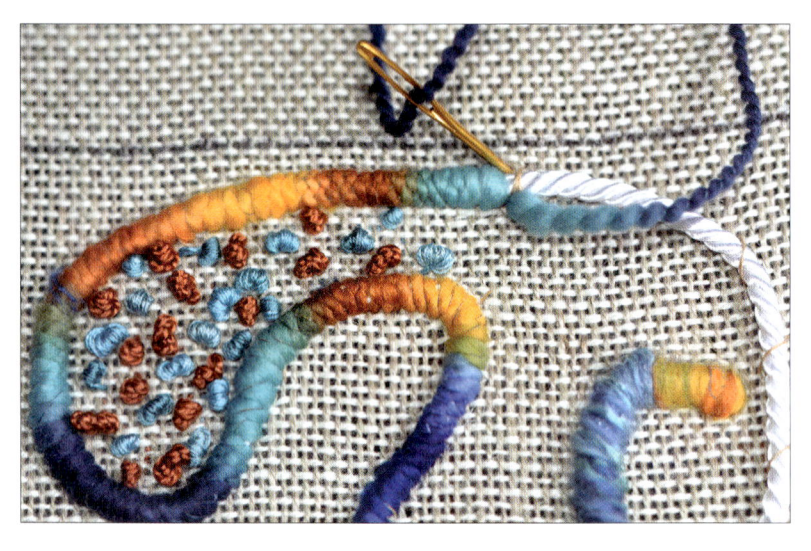

Anne embellished her work with French knots or bullion knots.

A colorful netting was used to create a fisherman's catch.

Beading

After attending a gem show with her jewelry designer daughter several years ago, artist Cindy Irwin discovered the world of gemstones and has used them in her work ever since. Embellishing rug hooking with her "gems" allows her to combine her two passions. She wires the gemstones onto the backing with jewelry wire and crimp beads before the hooking is done.

Madison's Fairy, 26" x 31", #1- to 8-cut wool, sparkle Lurex wool, polyester fabric, pyrite, pearls, and crystals on linen; traditional rug hooking and beading. Designed by Lenny Feenan. Hooked by Cindy Irwin, Lancaster, Pennsylvania, 2014.

Madison's Fairy is a tribute to Cindy's granddaughter. The beach is embellished with pyrite, the flowers with pearls, and the sky, hooked with sparkle wool, also twinkles with hundreds of crystals. The glittery outline of the wings was achieved by affixing a transparent fabric to the wool with a spray adhesive and then cutting it out and hooking it.

Weaving

Tulip Splendor, 22" x 23", #8-cut wool, sari silk, and yarn on linen; traditional rug hooking, tapestry weaving, and standing wool circles. Designed and hooked by Becky Jackson, Lakemont, Georgia, 2014.

Color and fiber have always made Becky Jackson's heart sing. Through the years she has enjoyed embroidery, sewing, needlepoint, knitting, tapestry weaving, and of course, rug hooking. Her inspiration for *Tulip Splendor* was a tapestry piece she had already woven, and technically, in this case, her rug hooking embellishes the weaving. She wanted her piece to burst with color from the inside to the outside. Wool strips, novelty yarns, and sari silk were incorporated as well as a few standing wool circles for extra interest. The direction of her hooking, which radiates out from the tapestry, beautifully produces the effect that she wanted to achieve.

Knitting

Moss, 15" x 13", hand-cut wool, cotton, synthetic fabric, and yarn on monk's cloth; traditional rug hooking, knitting, crochet, prodding, and embroidery. Designed and hooked by Tracy Jamar, New York, New York, 2010. TRACY JAMAR

One early spring, as the countryside came alive with a myriad of greens, Tracy Jamar decided to create a tribute to moss. She used the opportunity to experiment with a monochromatic color scheme as well as several textile techniques in one project. She combined traditional rug hooking with knitting, crochet, prodding, and embroidery. The knitting is the grayish green curved swath that rises upward and curls over itself. She crocheted around the edges, especially on the right side and on the bottom.

Spool Knitting

Spool knitting is a form of knitting that uses a spool and a number of nails to produce a narrow tube of fabric. It is a technique often used to teach children the basic principles of knitting.

Labyrinth, 19½" x 20", #6-cut wool, roving, and yarn on linen; traditional rug hooking, spool knitting, and needle felting. Designed and hooked by Marilyn Bottjer, Eastchester, New York, 2013. JOHN BOTTJER

Labyrinth satisfied Marilyn Bottjer's innate love of geometrics and working with white. The labyrinth outline is spool knitted. She needle felted the brownish weed clump in the lower right corner.

Appliqué

Appliqué is a needlework embellishment technique in which pieces of fabric are attached to another surface, adding contrast of color or texture.

Purple Reign, 28" x 28", hand-cut wool in various widths and buttons, glass beads, and rayon floss on monk's cloth; traditional rug hooking and appliqué. Designed and hooked by Tracy Jamar, New York, New York, 2009. TRACY JAMAR

In *Purple Reign,* Tracy Jamar experimented with how fabric transforms when hooked. Next to each unhooked, appliquéd piece of fabric is a section that is hooked with the same fabric. The flat appliqué was outlined with sashiko stitches. Buttons and beads were added for texture and interest.

Combining Different Needle Arts | 55

Quilting

Furrows, 34" x 23", hand-cut wool and cotton in various widths on monk's cloth; traditional rug hooking, appliqué, and bias shirring. Designed and hooked by Tracy Jamar, New York, New York, 2014. TRACY JAMAR

In *Furrows,* Tracy Jamar used vintage wool challis quilt squares as her inspiration. Some of her squares were made like log cabin quilt squares. A strip was sewn to the foundation, folded over to hide the raw edge, and then another was sewn over that next raw edge, folded over, and so on. The wavy bars are an example of bias shirring.

Trapunto

Trapunto (Italian for "to quilt") is puffy and decorative. It is one of my favorite techniques because it allows me to use fabrics that are not hooking friendly, such as silk brocade.

Detail of Dupioni Prodded Sunflowers.

In *Dupioni Prodded Sunflowers,* I cut two pieces of silk brocade, applied a seam sealant to the edges, stuffed them with dryer lint, and sewed them to the backing. I like to use dryer lint because it is softer than polyester fiberfill. See the full rug on page 35.

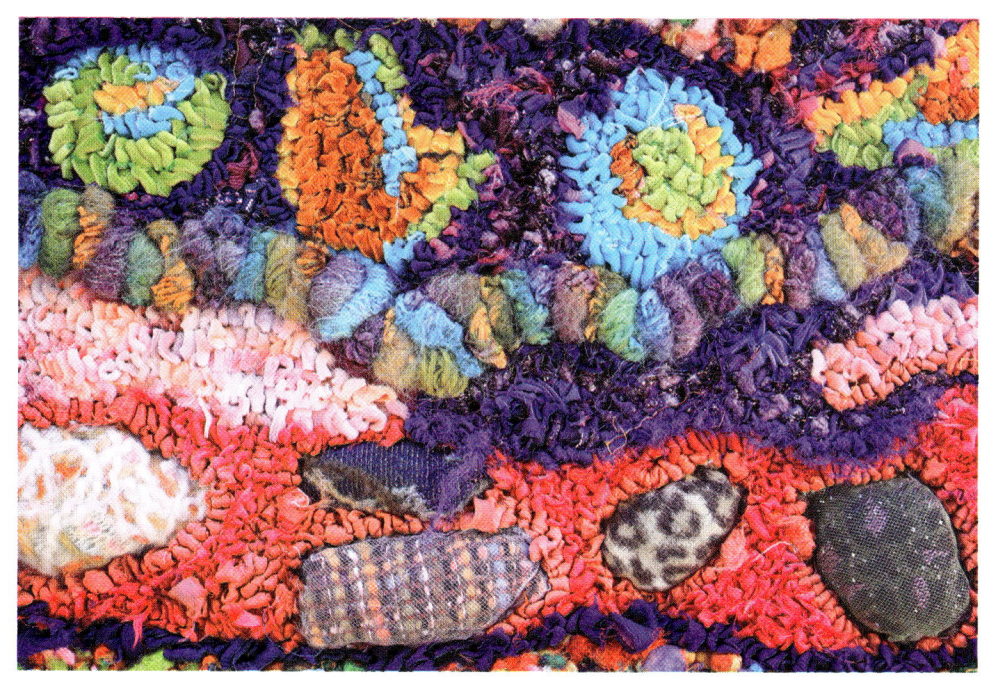

Detail of The Candy Store.

I used trapunto to showcase fabulous wool samples that I was given at Mood Fabrics. I loved the colors, but I never ordered any yardage because they tended to fall apart when I tried to hook them. Some continued to fray even after I sewed them, so I stitched sheer fabric over them to keep them intact. See the full rug on page 112.

Ruching

Ruching is a trimming technique that Corinne Watts achieved by using Pellon Fabric Magic, an interfacing material that adds texture and dimension. She made a bundle of three materials, with costume fabric on top, wool in the middle, and Fabric Magic on the bottom. She pinned these together and then machine sewed all over the top of the bundle. She then wet the bundle with a squirt bottle filled with water. The Fabric Magic shrinks when wet, bunching up, and the wool and the costume fabric bunched up with it. The result was a fabulous textured mass that looked exactly like a peacock breast. She cut the bundle to fit the area of the breast and sewed it to her piece.

When it is sewn onto other material and steamed, it shrinks up to 30%. The results are permanent and will last through laundering. She used it to ruche layers of wool and costume fabric to create her incredible peacock's breast.

Corinne said that the technique can be "as dimensional as you want by padding behind the 'fabric' once it is made. But, when it is flat on the piece, it is about the same height as the hooking around it. The technique would be great to use with a lot of padding—maybe in smaller amounts that direct your eye to move around a piece. Bottom line, this stuff has great potential to be used in many ways!"

If You Got It. . . . Flaunt It!, 31" x 44", #3- to 7-cut and hand cut wool, sparkle wool, lamé, sari silk, taffera, various coustume fabrics and braids on linen. Designed by Priscilla Debloom, hooked by Corinne Watts, Baton Rouge, Lousisiana, 2016.
SHARON TURNER

Corinne played with how dimensional the ruching should be. She decided that using it flat was best because she didn't want the breast to overpower the rest of the peacock. The breast is such a strong visual statement on its own that the viewer's eye immediately goes to it and everything else recedes.

Overall, the fabrics and yarns that Corinne used were selected for their color and texture. This required a great deal of creativity and "thinking outside of the usual hooking box." She looked for possibilities beyond her wool stash to get the visual effect that she wanted.

Left: Although the textures may not be obvious in the photo, the wools used are similar in color but very different in texture to provide interest and to accent the eyes. The largest section is a dark teal/black bouclé; the area around the eye is a dark teal glitzy wool. The overall area is cohesive but more interesting than if Corinne had used one piece of fabric. The white around the eye is a very soft bouclé yarn.

Bottom right: Detail of feather "eye." Corinne wanted the feathers to be both luxurious and light/airy. She incorporated plaid silk taffeta, chiffon, sari silk, and glitzy wools. In the "white" part of the feather, you see several different costume fabrics with a very pale lavender glitzy wool.

Combining Different Needle Arts

Dry Needle Felting

The Guardian, 40" x 28", #3- and 5-cut wool, roving, and various yarns on rug warp; traditional rug hooking and needle felting. Designed by Elizabeth Black. Hooked by Gail Dufresne, Lambertville, New Jersey, 2005.

In 2005, I paid a visit to renowned artist Elizabeth Black. I brought some of my work to show her what I had been up to, much of which was mixed media. When I called to tell her that I was going to stop back on my way home, she told me that she had a surprise for me. When I arrived at her house, she presented me with a drawing of five sheep and the wildest dog I had ever seen—a Bergamasco, an Italian corded herding dog.

I loved the design and could not wait to get back home to come up with a cool way to hook it. Even though by then I was designing my own work, executing one that Elizabeth designed just for me was really special. I knew that flat, two-dimensional work was not going to do justice to this exquisite design.

I hooked all of the sheep faces realistically, using #3-cut wool strips. I used very bumpy yarn that resembled popcorn to get the feel of fluffy sheep. The grass is a mixture of #3-cut wool strips and all sorts of yarns. I pulled the loops up to about 1" and then clipped them to make a thick grassy area under the front sheep and the dog. I hooked the water with a combination of #3-cut wool strips and many yarns, including Trendsetter Aura yarn to make the water glisten. It all fell into place very quickly, and the entire piece, including the painted sky, was finished except for the Bergamasco, who was still just a white silhouette.

When I complained over and over about not being sure how to hook him, Elizabeth unsympathetically suggested that I just put a black X through the dog with my Rub-A-Dub. I considered it. Finally I decided that the best way to get the look of this wonderfully messy looking, matted dog was needle felting. I felted separate plates in different sizes for his body and then alternately both felted and sewed them onto the backing. I first hooked his face with roving and then I needle felted yarns over top of it.

Diego and Luke, 19" x 28", #4- and 6-cut wool and wool roving on linen; traditional rug hooking and needle felting. Adapted from a photograph taken by Mattias Herrera and hooked by Gun-Marie Nalsen, Loveland, Ohio, 2014. MATTIAS HERRERA

Diego and Luke was designed to be a wonderful Christmas present for Gun-Marie Nalsen's grandson, Diego. She asked her son Mattias to take a photo of Diego and his dog Luke. Luke's and Diego's bodies are traditionally hooked.

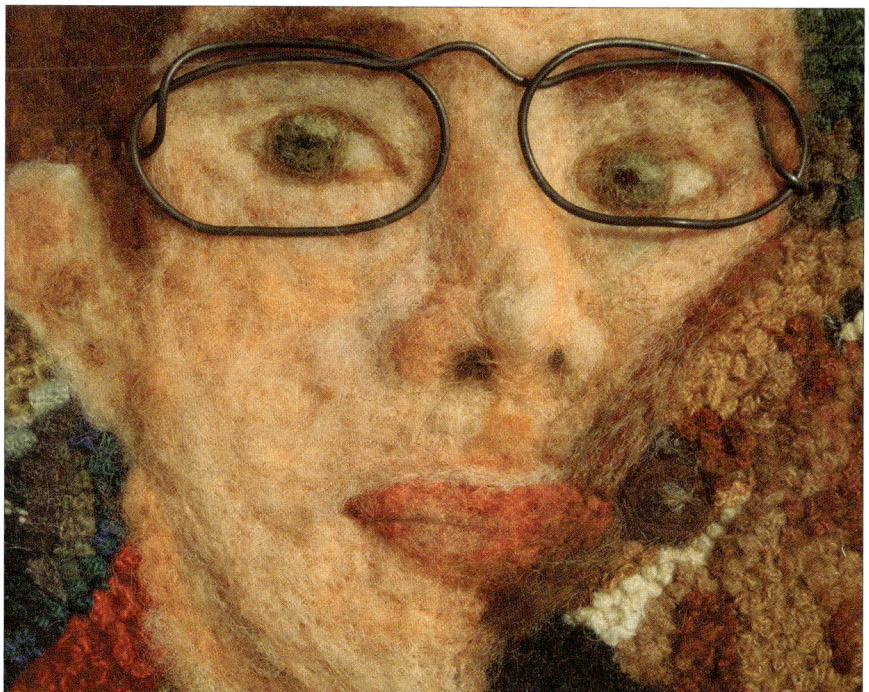

Detail of *Diego and Luke*

Gun-Marie made Diego's glasses out of wire, the finishing touch. She thought it might be easier to needle felt Diego's face, but found it to be quite a challenge in the application! The plaque is also needle felted and attached with wire.

Wet Needle Felting

Passion, 48" round, #4- to 6-cut wool, silk, and roving on linen; traditional rug hooking, braiding, and wet needle felting. Designed by Kris McDermet and Lynn Hoeft. Hooked and braided by Kris McDermet, Dummerston, Vermont, 2013.
KRIS MCDERMET

Kris McDermet is clearly not afraid to combine different needle arts. The concept for *Passion* grew from a wet felting class given by her friend Karen Kamenetzky. She first made the wet felted hearts and sewed them to the linen backing. She then hooked around them. She intentionally left open spaces around her braiding and hooking to allow the wall or floor where the pieces are placed to become a part of the design. The rug was made in eight different pieces and then sewn together at the end.

Detail of *Passion*

Crochet

Crochet is a popular finishing technique, one that Nola Heidbreder often uses. It works with either yarn or wool strips. If using yarn, Nola prefers to use chenille, bouclé, or thick eyelash yarn rather than multi-ply, plain yarn, as the latter tends to catch on the crochet hook and pull. If using wool, remember that crochet takes a lot of fabric. For one inch of crochet you will need at least twelve inches of fabric. Nola prefers thinner wool, such as Pendleton wool, rather than a herringbone or a loosely woven wool, and she usually cuts it in a #6 width and leaves it in long strips.

Happy Souls, 64" round, #6- to 8-cut and hand-cut wool and yarn leftovers, silk, wool coils, buttons, and stones on linen; traditional rug hooking and creative stitches. Designed and hooked by Anne Boissinot, Brampton, Ontario, Canada, 2014.
JULIANNE AUGUST

Anne Boissinot's inspiration for *Happy Souls* was the bottom of a shoe. She happened to casually look at her shoe sole and noticed that it had an interesting pattern. When she checked out other soles, she found similarly cool patterns. She photographed the sole, made a pattern, transferred it to linen, and hooked it with leftovers from other projects. She now regularly checks the soles of her friends' and family members' shoes looking for more inspiration!

Details of *Happy Souls*. The finished edges of Anne's souls are chain stitched close to the hooking.

Combining Different Needle Arts | 63

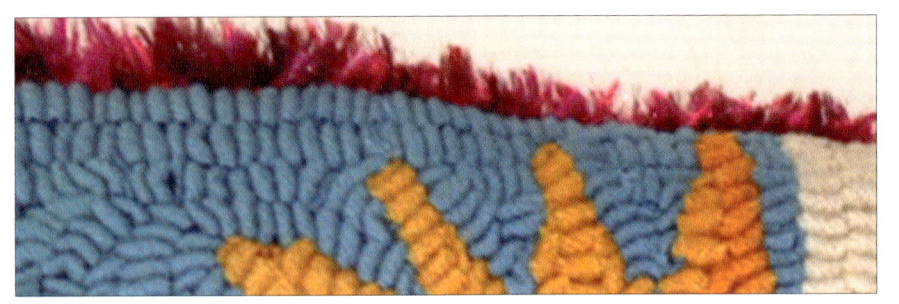

The edge of *The Sun Is Always Shining*. Crochet is a popular finishing technique and one that Nola Heidbreder often uses. It makes a great looking edge. For more information on this technique see Nola's chapter in the book *Finishing Hooked Rugs* (*Rug Hooking* magazine, 2013). See the entire rug on page 41.

Braiding

I have always liked to braid and have used it for years as an edge that I sewed on to my work rather than actual whipping. If I find an interesting yarn, or more than one yarn that would look good blended, I braid three strands and then sew the braid on to the edge. Or, for a shimmery edging or embellishment, why not try braiding with silk? It is especially effective with silk yardage, which can be challenging to hook because it frays. I used this effect in several of the response mats that I collaborated on. In *Time Flies*, I wound braided silk into spirals to represent flowers. I also used this technique on Anne Boissinot's response mat *Hand And Foot*, and on my response mat *What's For Lunch?*

CHAPTER 7

Combining Rug Making Techniques

As my rug hooking skills improved and my creativity expanded, I learned the rug making techniques of sculpting and prodding, which gave me two additional tools to add to my repertoire. Both techniques significantly influenced the evolution of my work. Now, I rarely hook an entire piece without using one or the other. A number of techniques work when combined with rug hooking. Let's take a closer look.

Sculpting

Waldoboro Floral with Teddy, 36" x 24", #3- and 4-cut wool on cotton; traditional rug hooking and sculpting. Designed and hooked by Jackye Hansen, Scarborough, Maine, 1990. GENE SHEPHERD

Shown here is Jackye's rug that depicts her husky and shepherd mix, her constant companion for 16 years. Jackie sculpted the prominent flowers in the wreath border in typical Waldoboro style.

When I began hooking in the mid-1980s, Jackye Hansen was one of my mother's favorite teachers. She specialized in, among other things, teaching the Waldoboro style of rug hooking and is considered a leading authority in this technique.

Waldoboro is a coastal village in Maine settled by German immigrants in 1740. Waldoboro-style rugs got their name from the rugs made by the ladies of Waldoboro from the mid-1860s through the early 1900s.

One of the two most distinctive features of these rugs is the technique of raising up and then clipping the loops to create a three-dimensional area within the design. The clipping, or sculpting, was referred to as "hoving," which gives a luxurious, velvety texture to the rugs. Sometimes the pile was as high as 3".

My first exposure to this type of hooking was when my mother and my sister took Jackye's Waldoboro class that specialized in hoving animals. My mother sculpted my brother's bull mastiff, and my sister, her son's Shar-Pei. The dogs were the central motifs, surrounded by another distinctive feature of the Waldoboro designs: a wreath-like scrolled border.

I do not remember when I started to incorporate sculpting in my rugs, but from then on, pretty much anything I hooked featured sculpting somewhere. It is time consuming and uses a ton of wool, but it is a very effective technique. Think of it as an enhancement for a traditionally hooked rug and an excellent way to highlight an important design element.

Four of Spades, 18" x 28", #4-, 6-, and 8-cut and hand-torn wool, silk, nylon, and glass eye on linen; traditional rug hooking, sculpting, and twisting/wrapping wool. Designed by Carol Feeney and Patti Ann Finch. Hooked by Patti Ann Finch, Medford, New Jersey, 2003. DEANNE HIGGINS

Patti Ann Finch, like me, is a big fan of sculpting. She participated in Linda Coughlin's international fiber exhibit, "The Art of Playing Cards." Artists selected a playing card to hook, and then all of the completed cards became part of a traveling art show. She and her mother, Carol Feeney, had fun working out a garden theme for the card she selected, the four of spades. Patti Ann sculpted a perfect sun, which beautifully demonstrates how effective sculpting can be to highlight a design element.

Self Portrait, 9" x 12", various cuts of wool, yarns, and butterfly pin on linen; traditional rug hooking, sculpting, and beading. Designed and hooked by Gail Dufresne, Lambertville, New Jersey, 2011.

In my *Self Portrait,* the little frog friend on my head is sculpted.

Combining Rug Making Techniques | **67**

Kentucky Montage, 36" x 27", #3- to 8-cut wool, various yarns, and novelty fabrics on linen; traditional rug hooking and sculpting. Designed by Melissa Elliott. Hooked by Gail Dufresne, Lambertville, New Jersey, 2010.

In *Kentucky Montage*, the little fish in the river was sculpted in a bright yellow wool not used anywhere else to pull the viewer right into the center of the scene.

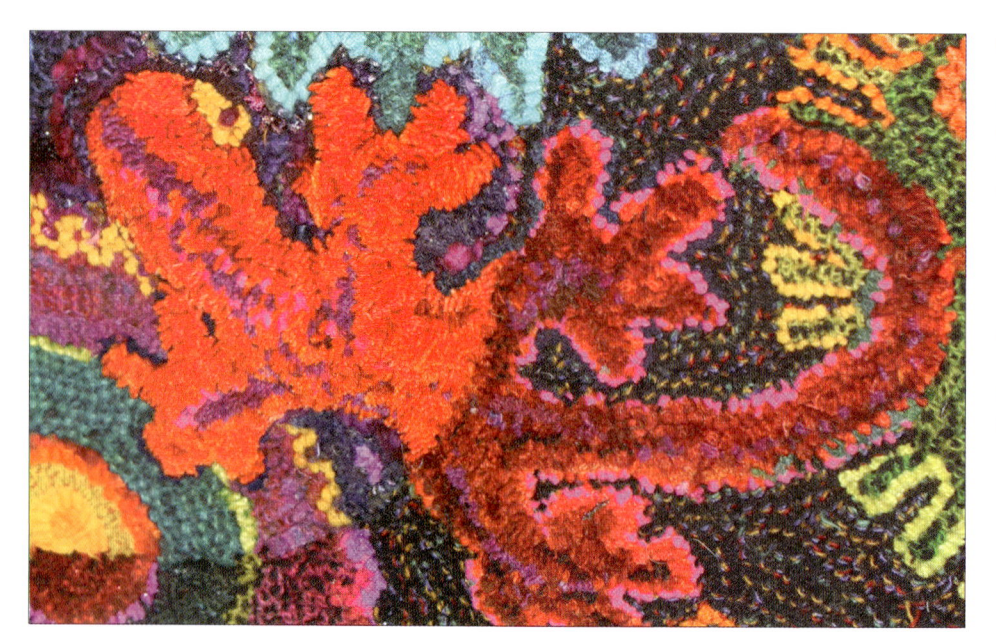

In *Gears,* the gecko is a design element used to bring the viewer's eye to the all-important arc of the circle that was created by the strategic use of values. He overlaps that arc and is highlighted by the use of a distinct color—bright red within the circle, darker red outside the circle—and by the technique of sculpting, which literally brings him closer to the viewer than the rest of the design.

Gears, 18½" x 22", #3- to 8-cut wool, various yarns, and sari silk on linen; traditional rug hooking and sculpting. Designed and hooked by Gail Dufresne, Lambertville, New Jersey, 2012.

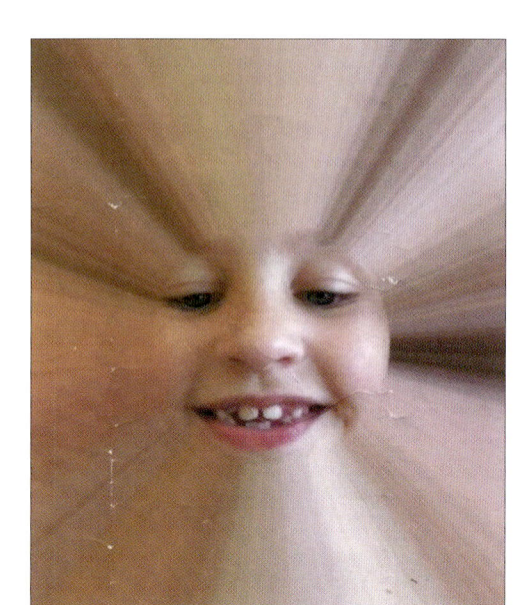

The original, manipulated photo.

Lillie, 12" by 12", #3 and 4-cut wool on monk's cloth. Traditional hooking and sculpting. Designed and hooked by Katy Prescott, Baton Rouge, Louisiana, 2016.
SHARON TURNER.

Artist Katy Prescott, a relatively new rug hooker but longtime fiber artist, immediately took to the technique of sculpting and incorporates it into most of her work. In this piece, she sculpted a selfie taken by her then 5-year-old granddaughter, Lillie.

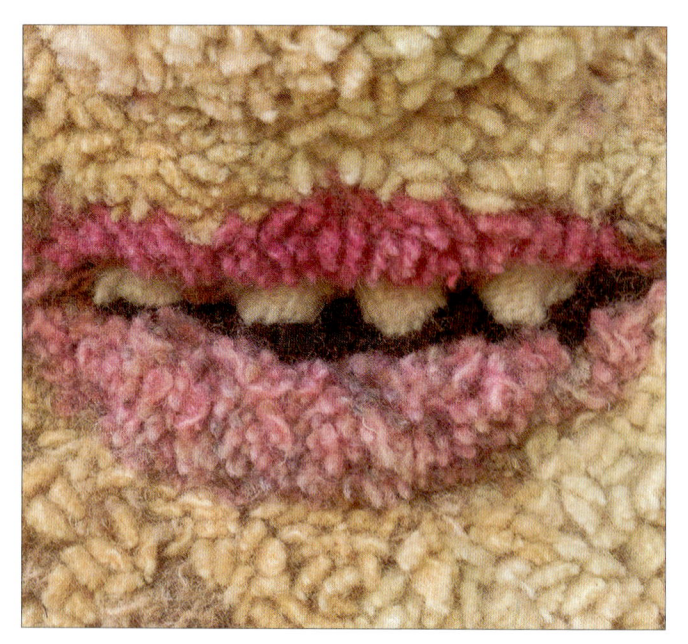

Lillie's teeth are even sculpted.

The eyelash wool was pulled up high and then clipped to different lengths.

70 | Rug Hooking with Fancy Fibers

Flamingos, 25" x 36", #3- and 4-cut wool and various yarns on linen; traditional rug hooking and sculpting. Designed by Elizabeth Black. Hooked by Gail Dufresne, Lambertville, New Jersey, 2005.
All three of the flamingos in this Elizabeth Black design are sculpted.

Combining Rug Hooking Techniques

Prodding

Proddy Lion, 20" x 22", #3-cut to 1"-cut wool and various yarns; traditional rug hooking and prodding. Designed and hooked by Gail Dufresne, Lambertville, New Jersey, 2005.
My proddy lion is one of my first prodded pieces. I honestly couldn't imagine hooking his mane on the same plane as his body. The face was hooked in #6 cut, the eyes were hooked in #3 cut, and the background is #8 cut. I prodded the mane with about 10 different plain and textured wools in #10 cut or hand torn strips.

Prodded mats were first made hundreds of years ago in the United Kingdom to cover bare floors and ward off the chill, just as our country's traditional hooked mats were originally designed to do. Like our traditional mats, most designs were simple and were made out of any fabric scraps that could be found.

I was introduced to prodding in the 1990s at the Green Mountain Rug School where English artists Heather Ritchie and Cilla Cameron were teaching the technique in adjacent rooms.

Two distinctively different methods are used to prod. If using the wooden peg type tool, strips of wool are poked through the side of the backing on which the design is drawn. What we think of as the back of our hooking becomes the front of the rug, where the completed design is. Any tool that can poke strips through the backing can be used, including a hook for rug hooking. The backing should be held taut on a frame or hoop.

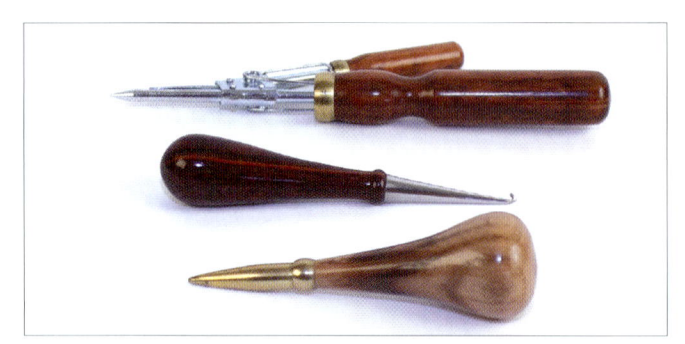

There are various types of tools used for prodding, such as the spring-loaded proddy tool, peg tools, and the Miller hook with fat shank, shown above.

The one I prefer is spring loaded and resembles a curling iron. It is used on the same side of the rug as the design is drawn, and the technique is more easily done without a frame or a hoop.

After I prodded the mane, I hooked through it with a funky yarn with bits of roving that looked like fur.

Big Sheep Face, 21" x 16", #3- to 10-cut wool, wool yardage, and various yarns on linen; traditional rug hooking and prodding. Designed and hooked by Gail Dufresne, Lambertville, New Jersey, 2007.

To get the effect that I wanted for the top of the head and neck of my *Big Sheep Face*, I tried first to prod using my spring-loaded prodding tool and ½" strips of wool, but the result was just not what I wanted. So I used my regular hook to pull loops in a variety of cuts. I pulled these significantly higher than the face, at varying heights. I clipped some of the higher loops and left others looped.

Prodding Flowers

Prodding flowers gives them the three-dimensional look they deserve. One of my favorite flowers to hook is sunflowers. Once I discovered prodding and sculpting, I never hooked another flat flower.

Large Proddy Sunflower, 27" x 43", #3- to 10-cut wool, silk, and various yarns on linen; traditional rug hooking, prodding, sculpting, needle felting. Designed and hooked by Gail Dufresne, Lambertville, New Jersey, 2008.

This large, lone sunflower has a needle felted center. How different it would have looked had I hooked it flat!

Cow and Sunflowers, 25" x 20", #3-cut to hand-torn wool and various yarns on linen; traditional rug hooking and trapunto. Designed and hooked by Gail Dufresne, Lambertville, New Jersey, 2005.
Cow and Sunflowers was one of my first prodded pieces. The flower centers are stuffed in trapunto style.

Prodding uses lots of material. The higher and wider the prodding, the more material needed. For this **Velvet Poinsettia**, with an 8" or 9" circumference, I used a full ¼ yard of velvet. The center is Dupioni silk stuffed with dryer lint, and sewn to the rug in trapunto style. I circled the center with hooking using sari silk and a glitzy yarn. Velvet has two very distinct sides. If you want the soft luxuriant side to be the top side, you need to manually arrange the petals after prodding to accentuate the soft, top side.

A wonderful example of a combination of prodded and traditionally hooked flowers is Chris Preble's *Wedding Crock Bouquet,* a design inspired by a personalized stoneware crock she gave to her eldest son for his wedding. She prodded several varieties of flowers and leaves in many different colors. She hooked some flowers by pulling the loops very high; others were hooked traditionally flat.

Combining Rug Making Techniques

Wedding Crock Bouquet, 20" x 25", #3-, 4-, and hand-cut wool, cotton yarn, and glass beads on linen; traditional rug hooking, prodding, and appliqué. Designed and hooked by Chris Preble, Jasper, Georgia, 2007. CHRIS PREBLE

Wedding Crock Hydrangeas, 19 1/2" x 23", #3-, 4-, and hand-cut wool and glass beads on linen; traditional rug hooking, prodding, and appliqué. Designed and hooked by Chris Preble, Jasper, Georgia, 2014. CHRIS PREBLE

When Chris's middle son married, she also gave him a personalized wedding crock and designed the accompanying *Wedding Crock Hydrangeas* for the lucky couple. She cut the hydrangea flowers from specially dyed lavender and green wool. She appliquéd individual flowers to a hooked base with thread and glass beads. This technique, according to Chris, "allowed the flowers to bloom."

Combining Rug Making Techniques | 77

Prodding and Portraits

Lindsey, 30" x 38", #4- and 8-cut wool on linen; traditional rug hooking, prodding, and appliqué. Designed and hooked by Margaret Wenger, Lancaster, Pennsylvania, 2009.

If Margaret Wenger hadn't prodded her granddaughter Lindsey's hair in this mat, but merely hooked it in two-dimensions, this piece would never have the powerful, unique effect that it does. The finished piece is large, and some of the wool strips Margaret used are as long as 6". The prodding perfectly frames Lindsey's face. Note the shape Margaret chose for the overall rug, mirroring the shape of Lindsey's head.

Actual photo selfie of Patti Ann

Selfie, 15" x 18½", #4-, 6-, 8-, and hand-torn wool, silk yardage, sparkle nylon fabric on monk's cloth; traditional rug hooking and prodding. Designed and hooked by Patti Ann Finch, Medford, New Jersey, 2013. DEANNE HIGGINS

For her self-portrait, Patti Ann Finch used prodding not to highlight her hair, as Margaret did with Lindsey's hair, but to hide it! Patti Ann decided that her first piece would be her own selfie so that no one would be offended if it did not turn out well! She also liked the idea because it was a timely topic—everyone at the time seemed obsessed with "selfies."

Patti Ann always wears her hair up and worried how it would look hooked traditionally. While she was taking her photo in the backyard, she noticed a beautiful crepe myrtle in full bloom. She stuck her head into the bush and snapped the selfie! The prodding perfectly frames Patti Ann's face, and the gorgeous color, which is Patti Ann's favorite, gives a wonderful zing to the whole project. I can't think of any way that traditional hooking could enhance Patti Ann's face the way this prodding does.

Actual selfie of Macy

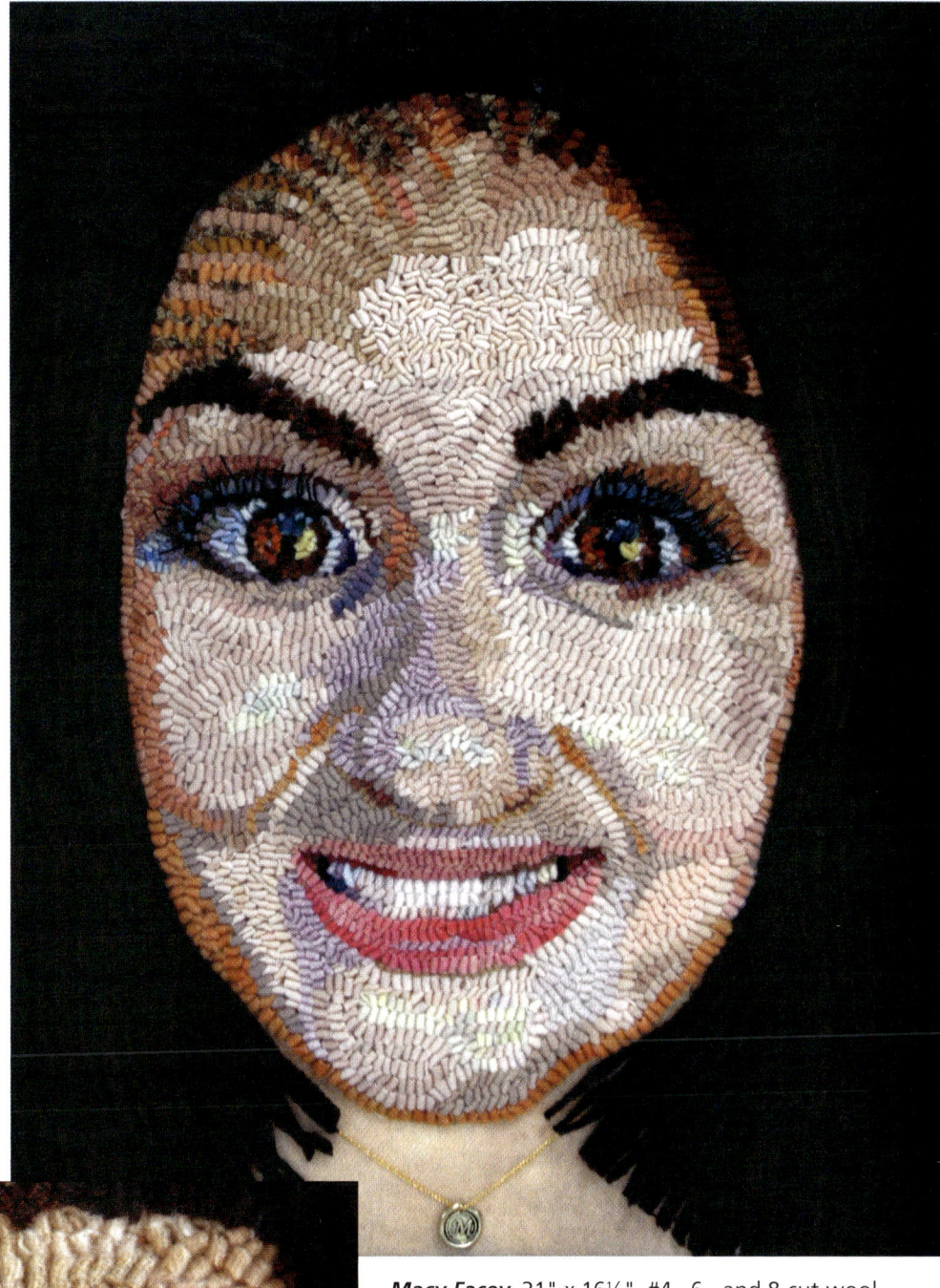

Macy Facey, 21" x 16½", #4-, 6-, and 8-cut wool, velour, black wire, and pendant on monk's cloth; traditional rug hooking and appliqué. Designed and hooked by Patti Ann Finch, Medford, New Jersey, 2014. DEANNE HIGGINS

After Patti Ann's 18-year-old daughter, Macy, saw Patti Ann's selfie, she begged Patti Ann to hook one for her. Macy has gorgeous eyes with very long eyelashes. Patti Ann spent a good 10 hours just hooking those eyes! She sewed wool flat to the backing to represent Macy's long, straight, black hair, which is a perfect frame for Macy's face. She used black wire for Macy's eyelashes and attached a pendant with an M. That's Macy!

Combining Rug Making Techniques

Eye Chart, 29" x 17", #3-cut and hand-torn wool and novelty yarns on linen; traditional rug hooking and prodding. Designed and hooked by Gail Dufresne, Lambertville, 2008.

Eye Chart is my response to having been asked to teach how to hook different eyes. I hooked all the eyes on one piece of linen and then connected them by prodding the negative space with various wools and yarns. The result has been referred to as "creepy." I agree!

Braiding

For as long as I can remember, braided borders have been made for traditionally hooked rugs, and I have always loved the look. Patty Mahaffey offered to teach me to braid. I bought all of the braiding equipment she recommended and selected the materials. Each week, she came to my Saturday classes and noticed that I had not even taken a stab at the braiding. Finally, she took the three wools I used to bead the perimeter of *Lizzie* (in the gallery) and added a braided border to a prototype I had hooked of one of Lizzie's circles.

Patty's Mat, 10" diameter, various cuts of wool and yarn leftovers on linen; traditional rug hooking and braiding. Designed and hooked by Gail Dufresne, Lambertville, New Jersey; braided by Patty Mahaffey, Perkasie, Pennsylvania, 2012.

This piece is very special to me because Patty passed away far too early and I miss her every day. I never did learn to braid. I am pleased to have this little mat as a memento of a cherished friendship.

The Greeting, 59" x 74", #5- to 7-cut wool on linen; traditional rug hooking, braiding, and trapunto. Designed, hooked, and braided by Kris McDermet, Dummerston, Vermont, 2009.
KRIS MCDERMET

Kris McDermet is a master at combining braiding with traditional rug hooking and, in fact, coauthored a book on the subject. She has been hooking and braiding for over 30 years. She fell in love with making combination rugs when her braiding teacher mentioned that sometimes a braided row of border was added to a hooked rug. She now loves to experiment with making interesting hooking and braiding combinations.

Kris's inspiration for *The Greeting* came during a trip to New Mexico, where she learned about an aboriginal group that begins each day by facing and greeting the sun. The mini braided rug in the center of the turtle's back is stuffed with wool, raising it, to represent the fact that in some native countries the turtle carries the weight of the world on its back. The border contains the geometric design that when extended forms the classical seven circuit labyrinth. The finished piece includes nine borders of hooking and braiding.

Combining Rug Making Techniques | 81

Braided Strawberry Rug, 27" round, #4-cut wool strips on linen; traditional rug hooking and braiding. Designed and hooked by Barbara O'Connell, Feasterville, Pennsylvania, 2014.

One of my newest students found a way to combine traditional rug hooking and braiding without actually braiding. She bought an inexpensive braided rug that matched the color scheme of her hooked rug, removed the center of the braided rug, and replaced it by sewing in her hooked rug. Pretty clever!

Punch Needle

Fish Deco, 21" x 16", #7- and 8-cut wool and cotton thread on linen; traditional rug hooking and creative stitches. Designed by Anne-Marie Herrera and hooked by Gun-Marie Nalsen, Loveland Colorado, 2012. MIGUEL HERRERA AND ANNE-MARIE HERRERA

Punch needle and traditional rug hooking have been closely connected for years. Gun-Marie Nalsen's spectacular *Fish Deco* is a wonderful example of combining these two techniques. Ah, the colors! This was a piece especially created for the "School of Fish" exhibition in Cincinnati. Gun-Marie hooked the body in black and white squares (so much for that old rule of never using pure black and white!). She punch needled the head, fins, and tail with cotton thread. The fins and the face were stuffed, and then the entire fish was cut out and mounted on small wooden cubes to give the impression that it is "floating" on the black background. Not surprisingly, this piece took the first place blue ribbon for mixed media at the Ohio State Fair.

Combining Rug Making Techniques

Standing Wool Circles, or Quilling

The simple but extremely addictive technique of rolling wool into circles and then somehow adding them to your traditional rug hooking has become very popular. Once I started making them, I couldn't stop! I did nothing but make them for days on end, and they fostered loads of new design ideas.

San Antonio Sunflowers, 15" x 11", #8-cut and hand-torn wool and various yarns on linen; traditional rug hooking, standing wool circles, and trapunto. Designed and hooked by Gail Dufresne, Lambertville, New Jersey, 2014.

The rolled circles originate from another style of rug making called standing wool rugs. Also called rolling wool or quilling, the name refers to the Victorian paper craft with the same name. Those little (and not so little) circles pop up in many of the works featured in this book. They can blend into the background to add a subtle surprise or, as in *San Antonio Sunflowers,* which was designed to be a mixed media teaching sampler, they can make a border really pop.

Standing wool circles

Quill Fantasy, 20" x 14½", #7- to 8.5-cut wool on linen; traditional rug hooking and quilling. Hooked and designed by Rita Vail, Green Valley, Arizona, 2012. LARISA VAIL

Rita Vail is a master at quilling and has created her own unique quilling technique. The result of Rita's experimentation is a perfect example of what happens when you allow yourself time to play. *Quill Fantasy* showcases her own fabulous style of quilling. The flowers begin with quillies in the center and then dribble into a garden of color. She added leaves and stems along the way, and last, she quilled the sky. Notice that Rita even signs her work in her own distinct quillie style.

Quillies can blend into the background or add a somewhat subtle surprise, as in this leaf.

In **Square Mixed Media Log Cabin** and **Rectangular Mixed Media Log Cabin,** quillies replace the traditional log cabin chimneys, or centers, of the blocks. With a little button embellishment in **Rectangular Mixed Media Log Cabin with Buttons**, the quillies become even more special.

Quill Blue Agave, 11" x 43½", #7- to 8.5-cut wool on linen; traditional rug hooking, quilling, and braiding. Designed and hooked by Rita Vail, Green Valley, Arizona, 2013. LARISA VAIL

Rita lives in the Sonoran Desert and loves cactus and other desert plants. In *Quill Blue Agave,* she quilled the yellow flowers and plant leaves and braided the trunk to emphasize its rough texture.

Detail of Quill Blue Agave

Combining Rug Making Techniques | 87

Quillie Loon Under Aurora Borealis, 16" x 20", #8.5-cut wool on linen; traditional rug hooking and quilling. Designed and hooked by Rita Vail, Green Valley, Arizona, 2014. MIKE LAROI

In *Quillie Loon Under Aurora Borealis*, Rita first quilled the loon and then progressed to the turbulent waves. She chose a Montana Aurora Borealis nighttime sky, not just for its beauty, but also because it is at night that loons are most verbal out on the water calling for a mate.

Quillie WHO Owl, 17" x 17", #7- to 8.5-cut wool and rug yarn on linen; traditional rug hooking, quilling, punch needle, sculpting, and proddy. Designed and hooked by Rita Vail, Green Valley, Arizona, 2014. LARISA VAIL

Inspiration for Rita's *Quillie WHO Owl* came from her collection of owl photos that she took in Montana. She drew the owl and pine branches on the backing and completed the quilling. Next she sculpted the owl's face and hooked the owl and the branches. She then reversed the backing and punch needled the sky and clouds. Last, she flipped the linen again and prodded the pine needles.

Rita's work inspired me to come up with my own standing wool circle technique. Using my sheep muse yet again, I created all sizes and shapes of standing wool circles to fit into the line drawing of the top, ears, and body of my sheep.

It took me a long time to make all of these pumpkin teeth, but the effect was worth it. Many onlookers are taken aback simply because the pumpkin is pink. Maybe it's time to cultivate a new pumpkin variety?

Shirring

Shirred rugs are made by gathering strips of material and then sewing them to a foundation. Only the sewing thread pierces the foundation fabric. Several variations of shirring are used, and although it is certainly not a new rug making technique, shirring is more recently being combined with traditional rug hooking, due in large part to Tracy Jamar, who co-wrote an excellent resource book about American sewn rugs. For more information on these types of rugs, I highly recommend *American Sewn Rugs: Their History with Exceptional Examples* by Jan Whitlock with Tracy Jamar (2012).

Hedgerows, 31" x 29" x 1½", various hand cuts on linen; traditional rug hooking, hand sewing, shirring, coiled wool, and appliqué. Designed and hooked by Tracy Jamar, New York, New York, 2011. TRACY JAMAR

Tracy's initial idea in *Hedgerows* was to create soft, horizontal lines, giving the impression of rolling hills receding into the horizon. She added free-form lines and spontaneously placed elements as the piece progressed. Tracy's interest in texture led her to use negative space as a design element. She left sections of the repurposed linen foundation exposed. The fuzzy beige line with some green and red/orange is a variation of chenille shirring. She unraveled rag carpeting and pulled it up tightly, as she would have done if it had been solid fabric. The technique is the same as conventional chenille shirring with just a small change in material. The lightest row of frayed material, under the swath of solid red, is not shirred; instead, it is strands of linen that were hooked through the foundation.

CHAPTER 8

Looking for Inspiration

If you want to learn about and work with mixed media, think about how you can expand your knowledge beyond traditional rug hooking. Explore all needle art techniques and dabble in other artistic endeavors. Exposure to other mediums will allow you to expand your own rug hooking horizons.

Inspiration From Other Artists

One way to find out what others are doing is to subscribe to publications such as *Cloth, Paper, Scissors* or *Fiber Art Now*. Both are dedicated to featuring mixed media artists and techniques and offer challenges to inspire fiber artists.

Another way to learn more is to join (or form) a group that includes artists who are accomplished in mediums other than your own. I recently joined a group called the Textile Study Group of New York (http://www.tsgny.org/). Members include a few rug hookers but also other artists who excel in all sorts of mediums. The group runs an online gallery in which members' work is featured, and it regularly posts challenges that members can participate in. Through an email list, its members are informed of upcoming exhibits.

The Sentinel, 8" x 21" x 8", various cuts of wool, wool roving, novelty yarn, embroidered wool felted balls, and pearl cotton on linen; traditional rug hooking and embroidery. Designed and hooked by Lucy Landry, Baton Rouge, Louisiana, 2013. LUCY LANDRY

Lucy Landry, an accomplished doll maker, attended my rug hooking workshop given to the members of The Contempory Fiber Artists of Lousiana. Like most of the participants, this was her first attempt at traditional rug making. As she was hooking waves and swirls of colors, she imagined a face peering out at her, as though from behind leaves in a jungle. "She was calm and steady, a silent witness in my studio. I added her in," said Lucy. She had a few felted balls that she had made previously that were just the perfect color, so she embellished them with embroidery and added them to her work. When the design was finished, she created a bolster pillow. She thought her finished work resembled a tree, one that surely must grow in some enchanted forest! Lucy hopes to continue with a series of bolster faces, which makes me happy to know that in some small way traditional rug hooking inspired Lucy to move forward in another endeavor.

Memories, 34" x 26", #4- and 5-cut wool, sparkly wool with Lurex, chenille yarn, and other various yarns on linen; traditional rug hooking, prodding, couching, and embroidery. Designed and hooked by Katy Prescott, Baton Rouge, Louisiana, 2014. SHARON TURNER

Katy Prescott, accomplished in all sorts of needle and fiber arts, grew up in a family that was accomplished in many types of hand work, but she had never hooked until our rug hooking workshop at The Contemporary Fiber Artists of Louisiana. Her inspiration for *Memories* was a tree that she passed each day. She especially admired the lichen on the trunk. The week after she photographed the tree, its owner cut it down!

The cattail stems were couched, and although they appear to be sculpted, Katy actually used an embroidery stitch to give them height and dimension. The hooked background dazzles due to the sparkly Lurex wool she selected.

Through another opportunity, I was asked to teach a beginning traditional rug hooking workshop to the members of The Contemporary Fiber Artists of Louisiana. All of the members of this group have varied skills and interests and excel in different mediums. They come together to inspire and to learn from each other. They invite teachers who are experts in diverse fields such as beading, doll making, embroidery, needle felting, quilting, and rug hooking so they can learn about new mediums.

My job was to teach these artists the basics of rug making, to arm them with another tool in their arsenal that could be incorporated into their own individual work. I knew going in that they were not necessarily interested in making an actual rug.

They picked up the basics in less than a day. Most began to randomly hook materials into their backing, with no particular design in mind. No one used a preprinted design.

I had brought a huge selection of wool and sari silk, and they were very interested in the silk. Most had used silk in their work before, so I set about demonstrating how to dye silk in the hopes of keeping their attention after I had covered the very basic technique of rug hooking!

Inspiration from Friends: Response Mats

You may have taken part in or at least heard of something called a "friendship mat." I have been involved in the creation of several of these projects over the years. Each member of a group decides to hook, usually in a specified area and/or with a specific subject matter, on a mat or mats. In some cases, the organizer will work out a theme or color plan ahead of time. The group may hook one mat, which may be destined to be a gift or a raffle rug, or each person may start a mat, pass their work in progress to another artist, and in the end, each participant winds up with a mat. Deborah Jones's rooster, hooked in one of the blocks on *Lizzie*, was originally designed to be hooked on a series of friendship mats.

Linda Coughlin and Burma Cassidy brought the concept of a friendship mat to a newer, higher level when they developed the "response rug," a collaborative effort designed to challenge the participants and expand the way in which each creates art. (Learn more in *Rug Hooking* magazine's June/July/August 2011 issue.)

Two Redheads Collaborate, Gail's Response Piece with Anne Boissinot, 18" square, #3-cut to hand-torn wool, novelty fabric, silk brocade, sari silk, beads, various yarns, zippers, and trinkets on linen; traditional rug hooking, sculpting, couching, trapunto, standing wool circles, and beading. Designed and hooked by Gail Dufresne, Lambertville, New Jersey, and Anne Boissinot, Brampton, Ontario, 2014.

Response Piece with Anne Boissinot

I created my first response rug when Anne Boissinot invited me to join forces with her. There were to be no rules, other than the fact that we agreed upon a mat size of 18" by 18" and that we would pick a mutually agreeable time to exchange mats.

The idea for the start of my mat came easily. Both Anne and I are redheads, so my idea was to position a redhead looking upward into the mat to forever admire our joint creation. I hooked her in and also outlined about two-thirds of the piece with the sari silk I was obsessed with at the time. I had no preconceived idea as to where this experiment was going to take us or what Anne's "response" might be.

When I got my mat back, a wonderfully vibrant, multicolored coil was couched just above my head, and my lush red yarn hair had been highlighted with purple yarn!

Anne had perfectly matched the level of intensity of my bright colors. Having collaborated on mats with others in the past, I knew how important it is to match the chroma (or intensity or brightness) of the work produced before yours. If you don't, the work in the higher chroma will overpower that of the lower chroma. This has always been my challenge when hooking with others: I usually need to tame mine down. It takes empathy to think outside of your own color and chroma preferences and pay close attention to the work of your collaborators. Clearly Anne understood this concept!

We made a date to exchange our mats a second time. I threw my mat over the back of my couch so I could study it each time I passed it and started to think about what I would do next. I still did not have any idea of a theme, and in fact, I never really did. My second response was nowhere near as forthcoming as my first. Now I felt pressure to match the quality of Anne's work. I wanted to make my work interesting, be creative, work out of the box, be fearless, and try new fibers and techniques.

My light bulb moment came just before our exchange was to be made. When I was in England, I bought some wonderful embellishments from India. Our response mat was the perfect project for some of them! I stuffed and sewed a few of my favorite velvets and novelty fabrics onto the mat in trapunto style and then sewed three of the Indian embellishments on top of the trapunto.

As I entered that blissful creativity zone, where ideas freely and fearlessly flow, I had trouble stopping myself because I wanted to make sure I left enough room for Anne to respond. I added a sheep pin to my hair. I added standing wool circles—the first time I used them in my work—and I hooked some of the negative space with all sorts of different fibers. Let's see what Anne had to say about that!

Anne's answer was, among other things, a jewel encrusted zipper! She also hooked a hand and embellished one of my standing wool circles with little clothespins. There was a spiral of beading and embellishments, such as a colorful little house trinket. I had to really study the piece to discover all that she had done.

It was my turn again. By this time, the ideas were flowing steadily and easily since the mat now had a "feel" to it, and Anne had responded positively to everything I had done. I no longer worried about how she would react and stopped putting so much pressure on myself. I never did think in terms of having a specific theme for this mat, and the only motif actually drawn on the mat was my initial redhead. I added a little frog key chain. I continued to fill in negative space with all sorts of fibers. The *pièce de résistance* was an ornamental zipper I found in New York City, an answer to the zipper she had added to my piece. I bought two, one for my mat and one for Anne's.

Anne worked last on my mat. When I opened the package, there hung the Eiffel Tower from the bejeweled zipper! Anne also added a beaded name tag.

Anne Boissinot's Response Piece with Gail: Hand and Foot, 18" square, #5- to 8-cut and hand-cut wool, silk, sparkly novelty fabric, yarn, velvet, corking, onion bag netting, shells, sand dollars, beads, necklace baubles, Lucille Ball watch face, stones, a glove, and other found objects on linen; traditional rug hooking, sculpting, cording, hooking high and low, quillies, embroidery stitches, corking, and beading. Designed and hooked by Anne Boissinot, Brampton, Ontario, and Gail Dufresne, Lambertville, New Jersey, 2014. JULIANNE AUGUST

Working Anne Boissinot's Response Piece: Hand and Foot

When I first received Anne's piece, she had hooked all sorts of fibers in one corner, and had sewn on a lovely piece of ceramic as an ornament. How to respond? Her work was not as bright, colorwise, as mine, so I toned my response down to follow her lead. I was timid in the beginning because, after all, this was not my piece, and I really wanted Anne to like what I did. I added some glitzy novelty fabric, some yarns, and a pretty purple bead.

Her response was to add shells covered with a mesh netting that looked like part of an onion bag from the grocery store. I responded with standing wool circles and French knots and some prodding. I noticed on this second exchange that both of us were climbing the chroma ladder. Her mat was progressively getting brighter!

On our next exchange I found a Lucille Ball watch face among the fiber! Anne had hooked a hand on my mat and I knew that she had hooked one on the mat she exchanged with Linda Coughlin. I had lost one of my favorite gloves and decided to sew the remaining glove onto her mat, in keeping with her "hand" theme.

When her mat came back, a foot had appeared, surrounded by a beautiful white area, definitely a beach. She had embellished that area with, among other things, a stone and a seashell. My first thought was that I had to balance that large expanse of white, and I did so by prodding around my red glove with a very pale whitish velvet. That and the mesh-covered white shells did the trick. I added pretty little embroidered mirrors that I found in my stash of embellishments from India.

Anne, like me, does not preplan her piece. As she sits to begin the process, she waits for an idea to come . . . she waits "until the muse is with me." Her creative challenge is to keep the piece balanced, both in color and proportion, and to know where to stop, which is surely something I struggle with. Her goal is to use these pieces to try out different materials and techniques.

Anne has collaborated on response pieces with several others. She found that each person had a different response style and that each person brought her own creativity. She loved seeing her partner's color choices and how she filled the areas. It was sometimes adventuresome, sometimes thoughtful, sometimes a total surprise. She notes, "A collaboration is not unlike a trust walk. You are spending time and energy doing the two pieces and trusting the other person." She wonders what her response partner will think when she sees her response. When she looks at the pieces, they say so much to her about the other person and herself and how they worked together to achieve balance, symmetry, and playfulness. The whole process becomes a close, creative, trusting relationship.

I just loved this creative process and how it gave me a chance to really get into Anne's head and see how she worked. Having a conversation with fiber rather than words is absolutely exhilarating! The process loosened me up and got me out of a terrible creativity rut that I had been in for some time. I found it to be the perfect format for trying out new ideas. I absolutely loved the camaraderie, playfulness, and creativity.

Anne and I have started a second round of response pieces because we enjoyed working with each other so much. I also asked several other people to play this creativity game with me, one of whom was Felicia Menin.

What's for Lunch?, Gail's Response Piece with Felicia Menin, 18" square, #3- to hand-cut wool, sari silk, velvet, lace, silk flowers, novelty fabric, silk brocade, various beads and buttons, onion bag netting, frog tile key chain, braided silk coils, embroidered sequins, various yarns, shells, and trinkets on linen; traditional rug hooking, sculpting, and beading. Designed and hooked by Felicia Menin, New York, New York, and Gail Dufresne, Lambertville, New Jersey, 2014.

My Response Mat with Felicia Menin: What's For Lunch?

I began my piece by sculpting half of a frog peering out from the right side of my mat, similar to the redhead that started the piece I hooked with Anne. I decided that the frog was thinking of a lady bug, and I sculpted the bug within a thought bubble.

Felicia ran with the concept that the frog was thinking about food and played with the idea of dinner options, adding question marks, exclamation marks, and other insect treats. I responded by sculpting a "paw" in the upper center of the mat—the frog trying to grab his supper?

Felicia hooked a lily pad and a lily, and I answered

by hooking the background as a body of water. Felicia hooked a lady bug trying to hide in the lower left-hand corner, expressing its dismay at being found. My response was to sew on part of a mesh onion skin bag to entrap that poor little bug. (I learned that technique from working with Anne!) I also added a glittery spider to the mix.

On her last go-round, Felicia got really wild with the embellishments. When I got my mat back, silk flowers were everywhere, as were buttons and critters and beads. The more she added, the more I added. We freely responded to whatever the other did, and just had a marvelous time!

My final addition was a frog tile key chain that Felicia had given to me some time ago for Christmas. It hangs from the frog's "paw."

Felicia Menin's Response Piece: Time Flies

Felicia Menin had established a theme for her piece before she started it. When her son was younger, he thought a lot about time and what it meant, so she wanted to depict the passage of time and incorporate new and old materials and mementos referencing moments in her family's life. When she and I exchanged mats the first time, she had at least one-third of the upper part of her mat already hooked in the most beautiful colors, and within what was an obvious sky, were watch hands set to times significant to members of her family, such as birth dates (including the birth date of her cat).

When it was my turn to hook, I added trapunto mountains from silk brocade and velvet. I found an embellishment that reminded me of Felicia's watches at M&J Trimming in New York City (a mecca of embellishments) and sewed it to one of the mountains. Felicia's response was to photo transfer images of land masses and create waves from trim that she found at M&J Trimming.

I answered with spirals I made from braided silk that represented flowers and hooked shimmering yarn around them to represent water.

Her final contribution was dried flowers that she had taken from an outdated hat, a sparkly embellishment to represent a reflection in the water, and a squiggle in the sky from a piece of her son's baby blanket.

Felicia's mat was easier to respond to because she had a clear theme, and even though there was little to no discussion about what we were going to do, I felt I knew where I should go. I did get to experience Felicia's joy when she saw what I had done. Anne and I missed much of that experience because usually our mats were brought to us by a third party.

Felicia Menin's Response Piece with Gail: Time Flies, 18" square, #3- to hand-cut wool, wool yardage, sari silk, velvet, watch faces, lace, silk flowers, novelty fabric, silk brocade, braided silk coils, beads, yarns, jewelry pieces, and shells on linen; traditional rug hooking and photo transfer. Designed and hooked by Felicia Menin, New York, New York, and Gail Dufresne, Lambertville, New Jersey, 2014.

Wanda Wallace and Gail's Response Piece: Great Time on the Islands, 18" square, #5- and hand-cut wool, sparkly wool with Lurex, sari silk, silk brocade, button, lizard pin, and stick on linen; traditional rug hooking, prodding, yarn bombing, and quillies. Designed and hooked by Wanda Wallace, North Bay, Ontario, and Gail Dufresne, Lambertville, New Jersey, 2014.

A Response Mat Designed to Be a Gift

Wanda Wallace and I decided to join efforts and create a response piece as a gift for our wonderful hostesses, Lolly and Jim Burnett-Herkes. Lolly and Jim live on Hinson's Island off the coast of Bermuda, where we stay each year on our annual trek to Bermuda to visit friends.

Wanda began our joint adventure. She was not sure where to start, but she tried not to overthink. She began to "yarn bomb" a branch that represented one I had found and loved on a Bermudian beach. Yarn bombing is a movement that started in Europe. Its purpose is to bring art, color, and fun to public places. Local knitters made brightly colored "sweaters" for trees and bollards in public areas. It's classified as a graffiti art form. What a great start to a gift for Bermudians and what a great format to experiment with a new technique!

Wanda traced the lines of the decorated twig onto the backing and then left that area blank so she could sew the twig in place after she hooked the sand and ocean around it. She also hooked a hibiscus, a flower that is everywhere in Bermuda and one of Lolly's favorites.

Then it was my turn, and I only had one turn. I strategically prodded all around the hibiscus because there was no more of the sparkly blue wool that Wanda used for ocean water or the pink spot-dyed wool she used for sand. I used trapunto to sew and stuff two masses of silk brocade: one that represented Bermuda and another for Hinson's Island. I attached a gecko pin to Hinson's Island because they are everywhere and Lolly loves them. I sewed two huge standing wool circles to the Bermuda mound to represent the one day that Wanda, Lolly, Jim, and I spent preparing meals for Meals on Wheels.

I then sent the piece to Wanda, who hooked a boat for the couple who have sailed around the world twice. She had a button that looked like a crescent moon so on it went. She used a wonderful sparkly wool for a perfect night sky.

Wanda enjoyed the element of surprise in working on this mat. She felt that the creative process was freeing yet challenging at the same time. She said, "It is important to try not to worry about what your partner thinks as this might stifle what you do. This was very hard for me. I was initially worried about what Gail would think of what I did. I had to let those thoughts go by the wayside and let creative thoughts seep in and take over. Trust is an important component of the joint effort. The anticipation of seeing what the other artist creates is half the fun."

My Response Mats with Bermudian Friends

Gail's Response Piece with Bermudians, 12" x 11", #4-cut to hand cut wool, sparkly novelty fabric, sari silk, silk brocade, book mark, sea glass, glass stones, buttons, and plastic lizards on linen; traditional rug hooking, appliqué, and Texture Magic. Designed and hooked by Gail Dufresne and many Bermudians; Gail Dufresne, Lambertville, New Jersey, 2014.

The concept of response mats is what gave me the idea of how to finish a little piece I started in Bermuda with a large group of fiber artists. About 20 of us sat around a table. We all had a small piece of backing. We were asked to hook a small area on our piece and then move it around the table so that all of the artists could hook a little on each piece. When we were done and I was back home, I connected all of the little hooked areas with sari silk that reminded me of the pink sand and turquoise water of Bermuda. I attached a book mark with a bit of beach glass that Wanda Wallace brought me from her hometown of North Bay, Ontario. I also attached a North Bay Ontario pin she brought me to a little felt heart. How great is it to have a place to keep and showcase mementos?

I was also experimenting with a fabric called Texture Magic at the time. It is a material that when stitched to other material and steamed, crinkles up into a fabulous brain-like texture. I attached it to several pieces of novelty fabric, added eyes, and attached it to the piece.

Mary Jean Whitelaw's Response Piece with Gail, 18" square, various cuts of wool, sparkle wool, and sari silk on linen; traditional rug hooking. Designed and hooked by Mary Jean Whitelaw, Belle Mead, New Jersey, and Gail Dufresne, Lambertville, New Jersey, 2014.

One of my favorite response pieces in progress is one that Mary Jean Whitelaw and I started together. Mary Jean began her mat by hooking a very realistic stink bug, an uninvited but frequent visitor to all of us here in New Jersey. My response took care of her bug.

Gallery

Traditional rug hooking is the common link in the exciting work showcased in this gallery. Look what these artists accomplished by combining rug hooking with other fibers and techniques.

Really Unusual Materials

Detail of *Checked Out*

Checked Out, 16" x 32" x 3" (in plexi box), shredded checks, machine size, paper, cotton thread, and linen on vintage linen; traditional rug hooking and machine sewn. Designed and hooked by Tracy Jamar, New York, New York, 2011.
TRACY JAMAR

Running her fingers through a pile of freshly shredded checks, Tracy Jamar thought it would be a shame to just throw them all out. She saw the check shreds as a diary of her financial past, and used them in *Checked Out*. She machine sewed the shredded checks to a vintage linen foundation, making a spiraling form suggestive of the ins and outs of her personal finances. The shredded dollar bills, which were used as a novelty packing material purchased years before, seemed to her to be the perfect surrounding for the checks, so she hand hooked them in a border around them. Even the piece of linen backing that Tracy used has shredded edges. "Money, money, money. . . . It's all about who has it and who doesn't, isn't it?"

Sea of Blue: Plastic Floats Forever, 52" x 40" x 4", various cuts, upcycled paper, and plastic (including the New York Times, telephone book delivery bags, feminine hygiene product wrappers, Easter basket stuffing, and ribbon) on linen; traditional rug hooking. Designed and hooked by Constance Old, New Canaan, Connecticut, 2009.
STEVEN BATES

Constance Old feels that using contemporary materials for the traditional technique of rug hooking creates an index of our time as well as a timeless piece. Paper and plastic interest her as abundantly available fibers that not only reflect the world that we live in today, but also, with imagination and coaxing, can be made into rugs or wall pieces. Living in an era of material excess, it intrigues her to work in a medium that originated from need and a scarcity of materials. She likes to experiment primarily with upcycled paper and plastic, which includes but is not limited to woven plastic tarps, disassembled polyester mesh bags, shopping bags, hand bags, and construction fencing.

Sea of Blue: Plastic Floats Forever was inspired by an article in *The Atlantic,* from which Constance learned that plastic is the first building material used by humans that does not sink. Plastic in water has a half-life of 500 years. Not only does it break down very slowly, but since it is less dense than water, it also floats forever on the surface as it breaks down.

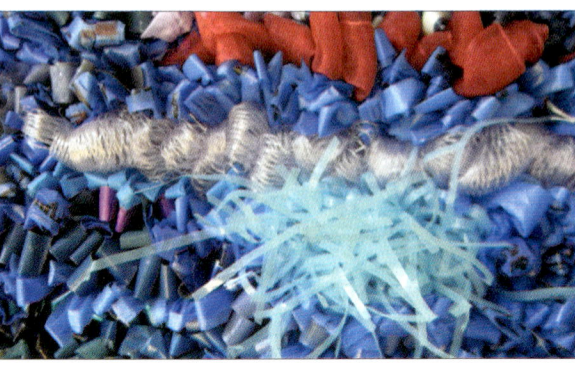

Sea of Blue: Plastic Floats Forever closeup.

Llama, 23" x 34", #6 and 8-cut wool, silk, linen, cotton, and novelty fabric on rug warp; traditional rug hooking. Designed and hooked by Margaret Wenger, Lancaster, Pennsylvania, 2014.

Artist Margaret Wenger is fearless in her use of color and fiber. All that fabulous depth of texture in the neck and face of *Llama* was achieved by using a combination of wool, silk, and cotton, which gives a depth of texture that wool alone cannot.

Liberace, 26" x 27", #6 and 8-cut wool, banana silk, silk, cotton netting, velvet, and novelty fabric on monk's cloth; traditional rug hooking and embellishing with banana silk. Designed and hooked by Margaret Wenger, Lancaster, Pennsylvania, 2012.

In *Liberace,* Margaret hooked some of the alternative materials higher than the rest of the hooking. The spectacular mane was achieved by hanging banana silk—yes, as in silk from banana trees!—loosely in long rows. And no trees were harmed, just trimmed a little.

Both *Liberace* and *Llama* are hooked on a backdrop of alternating black wool and black sparkly yarn. The color and the sparkle brilliantly set off both pieces and give the wonderful impression that they are floating in front of their backdrop.

Gallery | 103

Really Unusual Shapes

Lizzie, 64" x 84", #3- to 8-cut wool, sari silk, and various yarns on rug warp; traditional rug hooking, beading, and sculpting. Designed and hooked by Gail Dufresne, Lambertville, New Jersey, 2012. IMPACT XPOSURE

At 64" by 84", *Lizzie* is a big girl by anyone's estimate. She began as a friendship rug. A large group of us decided that we would each design our own rug and then allow each group member to hook a square on each rug. I drew 5" squares over the entire gecko design, to be filled in by friends. Before even one of my blocks was hooked, the group fell apart. What to do with a giant gecko? I turned many of the blocks into circles. I let a few blocks stay and filled them with sculpted motifs and shapes I thought were fun. I used colors and black and white for some high contrast and to break up the sea of green gecko. After I realized that this piece was not going to be passed around to members of a group, I thought it actually might be a great room-sized floor rug. The huge piece of rug warp that I drew it on was big enough to accommodate a rectangular rug that would have been about 8' by 10' to allow for *Lizzie's* undulating curves.

I had finished hooking Lizzie the gecko and had started hooking outside her shape when one of my students suggested I just stop with Lizzie. By this time, the rug had become so heavy and I had been hooking for so long that I jumped at this suggestion. I think the rug is far more interesting, and it has become my version of a bear rug. Only one person actually hooked a friendship block on my gecko: Deborah Jones hooked her trademark rooster at the end of the tail! My completed, revised *Lizzie* resides on my studio floor, but she would look spectacular as a focal point on a large wall.

Making Peace with Snow, 34" x 53", #4- to 7-cut wool, wool yardage, yarn, roving, antique glass buttons, and pearls on linen; traditional rug hooking and braiding. Designed and hooked by Kris McDermet, Dummerston, Vermont, 2009. KRIS MCDERMET

Kris McDermet is accomplished in both traditional rug hooking and braiding. She loves to experiment with making interesting hooking and braiding combinations, freely embellishing her work with both. In *Making Peace with Snow*, she hooked the lower scene in the woods first and then embellished it with braided centers to represent falling snow. The deer was hooked separately and then sewn on top of the foundation hooking. The yellow stars are embellished with antique glass buttons. She hooked each snowflake in the sky, packed and lined it, and then sewed it to the background, which is a piece of hand-dyed wool. She embellished all the flakes with antique glass buttons and yard sale pearls.

Inspiration from the Landscape

4 Seasons on the North Fork, 21" vertical when open; 7" x 5" (cards); 8" x 6" x 2¼" (box); #3-, 4-, and 6-cut wool yardage, felt, seaweed, and shells on burlap; traditional rug hooking and needle felting. Designed and hooked by Marilyn Bottjer, Eastchester, New York, 2007. JOHN BOTTJER

Marilyn Bottjer and her husband, John, have a second home on the North Fork of Long Island. Inspired by the changing light and look of the landscape there, Marilyn decided to hook postcard-sized pieces depicting the different seasons. She then created a box in which to store the postcards. She lined the box with felt and glued seaweed and shells to the inside bottom. The postcards fold down into the box. When the box is opened, the hooked postcards hang on a rod inserted into a wood base.

Shoreline 1, Mixed Media, 4½" x 6½", #6-cut and threads, leftover plain and texture wool, stones, beach seaweed, and Bermuda beach finds on linen; traditional rug hooking and needle felting. Designed and hooked by Anne Boissinot, Brampton, Ontario, 2014. JULIANNE AUGUST

I love these two beach scenes created by Anne Boissinot partly because they remind me of the wonderful Bermudian vacations she and I take every year with a group of friends. These pieces were actually rejects from another challenge. Anne came across them one day and decided to finish them. "I felt that I had nothing to lose so I began to play around using a strong fabric glue, and gut instinct, and I came up with two interesting pieces," Anne said.

She used wool, stones, shells, seaweed, and other Bermudian beach finds. The fabulous background in *Shoreline 1, Mixed Media* was accomplished by wetting a small brush and dipping it into blue dye and water, and then muddling it around the sky, water, and beach to obtain the feeling of a stormy sky that reflects on the water and beach.

Anne used 9" by 7" frames with black foam core from a dollar store as a base and then placed a smaller piece of foam core behind the hooked piece to add dimension.

Shoreline 2, Mixed Media, 4½" x 6½", #6-cut wool, threads, glass, wood, stones, beach seaweed, scrap of wire mesh, a piece of red material to represent a lobster, and tiny plant uprights on linen; traditional rug hooking and needle felting. Designed and hooked by Anne Boissinot, Brampton, Ontario, 2014. JULIANNE AUGUST

Gallery | 107

Through The Window #4: Fly Over Land Series, 20" square, various sizes hand-cut wool, cotton, silks, and yarns and fibers of unknown origin on monk's cloth; traditional rug hooking, appliqué with slight padding, and prodding. Designed and hooked by Tracy Jamar, New York, New York, 2010. TRACY JAMAR

While flying to visit family, Tracy loves to look at the land below and appreciate the beauty found in the variety of colors, shapes, and textures. "The unknown land connects me to my current and former home. The markings and layouts of the roads, farm fields, pastures, crops lines, lakes, rivers, and wooded areas show the effect humankind has had on the land. It looks quite lovely from a distance." *Through the Window #4* is the fourth in Tracy's *Fly Over Land* series.

Combining Needle Techniques and Fibers with Traditional Rug Hooking

Western Reserve Perennial, 19" x 23", #6- to 8.5-cut wool, sparkle wool, silk sari yarn, silk sari ribbon, silk sari chiffon, various yarns, roving, and handdyed rickrack trim on linen; traditional rug hooking, prodding, sculpting, beading, and standing wool circles. Designed and hooked by Linda Gustafson, Chardon, Ohio, 2014. LINDA GUSTAFSON

Linda Gustafson loves rug hooking, but she can hardly wait to finish the hooking and start the embellishing. *Western Reserve Perennial* began as a guild challenge. She knew right away that she wanted to make changes and embellish her version. Her goal was to use as many techniques as she could. The project evolved as she continued to work. The more she worked, the more ideas she got.

She prodded the large flower and made standing wool circles to represent the smaller flowers. She pulled her loops higher on the hill using wool and silk sari yarn. The stem is a piece of cording she wrapped with sparkle chiffon ribbon. The leaves are sculpted in wider cuts (#6, 7, and 8). She hooked the background in squares using wool, sparkle wool, silk sari ribbon, and silk sari chiffon. She beaded a beauty line between her background and her border. For the border, she sewed on roving that she braided and wrapped with contrasting eyelash yarn. She used silk sari yarn and silk sari chiffon and hand dyed sparkly rickrack trim for the outer edge.

Swamp Critters, 14" x 84", #6- to 8-cut wool, silk organza, mohair yarn, stones, glass, wood, buttons, shell beads, and feathers on linen; traditional rug hooking, prodding, sculpting, and beading. Designed and hooked by Corinne Watts, Baton Rouge, Louisiana, 2010. SHARON TURNER

Corinne Watts decided to respond to a call for entry for a gallery show at the Bluebonnet Swamp Nature Center in Baton Rouge. The show, *A Walk Through the Swamp*, included artwork by contemporary fiber artists of Louisiana. Each piece entered in the show was to be hung from the ceiling and visible from all sides as visitors walked through.

Her response was a long, skinny rug just over 1' wide and 7' long. She started from the bottom, drawing an alligator, an armadillo, three turtles, a heron, a raccoon, and an owl. "Each one revealed its own personality as they all came alive on the rug, and it was great fun to see how each developed," Corinne said.

Because the piece would be viewed from all sides, Corinne had to carefully consider how to finish the back. She chose a "camouflage" wool that actually has tree patterns woven into it, and she pieced the fabric so that one tree trunk ran the full length of the design. The completed piece hangs from wide tabs of camo wool that slide over a piece of swamp branch. Corinne liberally embellished her work with labradorite stones, glass, wood, shell beads, mohair yarn, and wool cutouts.

110 | *Rug Hooking with Fancy Fibers*

Aurora Borealis, 18" square, various cuts and hand-torn wool yardage, various yarns, novelty fabric, sari silk, silk brocade, and velvet on linen; traditional rug hooking, prodding, standing wool circles, and trapunto. Designed and hooked by Gail Dufresne, Lambertville, New Jersey, 2014.

I started *Aurora Borealis* with absolutely no idea as to where I wanted to go or what I wanted to create. It took on a life of its own, evolving as it progressed. I hooked and prodded with all kinds of materials. I stuffed and sewed silk brocade in the center and a black and white novelty fabric for the inner border. I liberally sprinkled in standing wool "circles" or tubes of all shapes and sizes throughout. I attached an embellishment I found at M&J Trimming.

The Candy Store, 30" x 22", #8- to hand-torn wool, various yarns, novelty fabric, sari silk, silk brocade, and velvet on linen; traditional rug hooking and trapunto. Designed and hooked by Gail Dufresne, Lambertville, New Jersey, 2014.

The Candy Store showcases favorite materials such as velvet, several varieties of sari silk, and pieces of material that were not "hookable" but that I could highlight with other fiber art treatments.

Purses

Many artists are combining traditional rug hooking with other mediums to create fabulous purses. Take a look at these confections and be inspired to make your own.

Purse #1280 2004, 9" x 10", various cuts of wool, mixed fiber yarns, cotton knits, and hand-covered buttons on monk's cloth; traditional rug hooking, crochet, and hand and machine sewing. Designed and hooked by Tracy Jamar, New York, New York, 2004. TRACY JAMAR

Purse #3617 2005, 9" square, various cuts of wool, mixed fiber yarns, panne velvet, cotton knits, silk, polyester, buttons, and glass beads on monk's cloth. Traditional rug hooking, crochet, hand and machine sewing. Designed and hooked by Tracy Jamar, New York New York, 2005. TRACY JAMAR

Gallery | 113

Alligator Purse, 15" x 13", various cuts of wool and buttons on linen; traditional rug hooking and sculpting. Designed and hooked by Corinne Watts, Baton Rouge, Louisiana, 2012. SHARON TURNER

Corinne Watts, a native of Baton Rouge, often draws from her heritage to find themes for her work. Her alligator purse is a great example. Many sections of the alligator are sculpted, and his eyes are buttons.

Purse #0629 2003, 7" x 6½", various cuts of antique paisley shawls, wool, mixed fiber yarns, panne velvet, cotton knits, silk, polyester, and antique buttons on monk's cloth; traditional rug hooking, crochet, and hand and machine sewing. Designed and hooked by Tracy Jamar, New York New York, 2003. TRACY JAMAR

Tracy Jamar thought it would be fun to make a variety of purses that she could use and sell. This endeavor allowed her to work with different color schemes and texture combinations without making a large commitment in time or materials.

Georgia Meets Gustav, 13" x 14", #4- and #6-cut wool, sparkle Lurex wool, leather, jade, amethyst, aventurine, amber, on rug warp; traditional rug hooking and beading. Designed by Jane McGown Flynn and Cindy Irwin, hooked by Cindy Irwin, Lancaster, Pennsylvania, 2014. CINDY IRWIN

In *Georgia Meets Gustav,* Cindy Irwin combined a Jane McGown Flynn design of an iris with her own Klimt-inspired design. On the iris side, she used amber to highlight the iris beards and aventurine to show the leaf veins. Over 700 amethyst beads were positioned in a swath starting at the top corner of the iris side and then fanned out to the bottom. The swath is repeated on the Klimt side. Cindy hooked the swath in a much smaller cut to accentuate it.

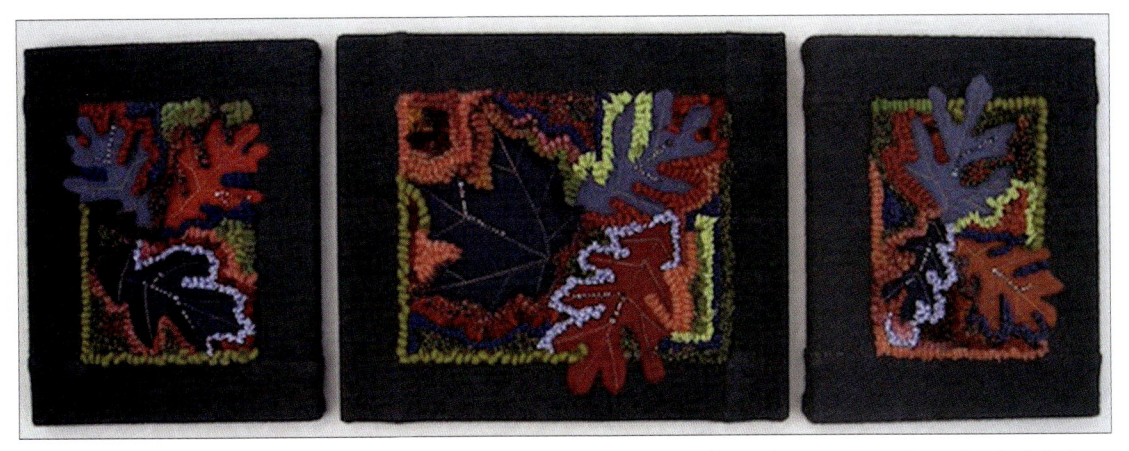

Leaf Triptych, 8" x 10", 12" x 10", 8" x 10", various hand-cuts of wool, cotton, and synthetic fabric, yarns, and glass beads on monk's cloth; traditional rug hooking with machine appliquéd leaves and hand-sewn beads. Designed and hooked by Tracy Jamar, New York, New York, 2007. TRACY JAMAR

Tracy's *Leaf Triptych* was designed to use up the leftover leaves designed for her purses. She stitched wool to the edges and wrapped it around a stretcher to give it a fabric frame.

Vases of Flowers

For many years, I have admired fiber artist Beth Kempf's work. I met her once, in 2015, at a rug exhibit in which we both had pieces on display, and there I got the chance to tell her what a fan I was. She has since passed away, but her outstanding, innovative contributions to fiber art live on.

Crock of Prodded Flowers, crock: 16" high by 8" in diameter, flowers various sizes and cuts of wool, wool selvedges, sari silk, novelty yarn, and buttons on linen; traditional rug hooking, standing wool circles, and prodding. Designed and hooked by Gail Dufresne, Lambertville, New Jersey, 2015. DICK OBERNDORFER

Since my current passion is standing wool circles, I wanted to incorporate this technique somehow. I also knew that I wanted to start with one tried-and-true technique that I know and love: prodding.

The centers of my flowers are standing wool circles. I prodded the flower petals and hid the very centers of the circle with a button, a bead, a little piece of glitzy yarn, or a piece of silk.

I hooked a simple leaf and a mirror image of that leaf so that I could glue them together to have a front and a back to wrap around a stem. I bought dowels for stems, but I really preferred the lumpy bumpy look of branches I found in the yard. I covered the stems with florist tape. On some, I also wrapped funky yarn around the tape for additional interest.

If you wish to see the original inspiration for my vase of flowers, check out Beth Kempf's web site: *www.happyrughooker.com*, where you will find her vase. Mine is not as exciting yet, but I have all sorts of ideas on how to expand on this idea. I have only just begun!

Proddy Vase Base, 12" x 12", #3-cut wool and yarn; traditional rug hooking, standing wool circles, and prodding. Designed and hooked by Gail Dufresne, Lambertville, New Jersey, 2015. DICK OBERNDORFER

Dragonfly Vase, Vase: 9" high, 9" circumference, flowers various sizes and cuts of wool, wool selvedges, sari silk, novelty yarn, and buttons on linen; traditional rug hooking, standing wool circles, and prodding, Designed and hooked by Gail Dufresne, Lambertville, New Jersey, 2015. DICK OBERNDORFER

I decided that the dragonfly vase needed a mat to rest on to make the piece look more complete, so I made a 12" square mat like the mat under my sheep *Jasmine*, using various cuts of all sorts of green wool. I hooked an area the size of the circumference of the vase for the vase to sit on so that it would not wobble. I hooked very high and unevenly, intentionally making it look messy, like a field of grass, and then randomly clipped loops. I worked my "glaze" of Trendsetter Aura yarn through the messy part. I left a small circular area unhooked and sewed a single prodded flower directly onto the linen.

Footstools

Quillie Sheep Footstool, 12" x 16", #3-hand cut wool, sparkle wool, sari silk, velvet, and novelty yarn on linen; traditional rug hooking, standing wool circles, and prodding. Designed and hooked by Gail Dufresne, Lambertville, New Jersey, 2016. DICK OBERNDORFER

Red Velvet Poinsettia Footstool, 9" diameter, hand-torn or cut wool, velvet, Dupioni silk, and sari silk on linen; traditional rug hooking, prodding, and trapunto. Designed and hooked by Gail Dufresne, Lambertville, New Jersey, 2015. DICK OBERNDORFER

Rectangular Mixed Media Log Cabin with Buttons Footstool, 12" x 16", #6-hand cut wool, sparkle wool, sari silk, novelty yarn, and button embellishments on linen; traditional rug hooking, standing wool circles, and prodding. Designed and hooked by Gail Dufresne, Lambertville, New Jersey, 2015. DICK OBERNDORFER

Jasmine on Her Grassy Knoll Footstool, 5½" x 3", #8-cut wool on linen (Jasmine) and 11" square, #3-cut wool, various yarns, and antique bobbins on linen (grassy knoll); traditional rug hooking and prodding. Designed and hooked by Gail Dufresne, Lambertville, New Jersey, 2016.
DICK OBERNDORFER

    I love footstool art. Footstools are easy to find and fun to hunt for at garage sales, thrift stores, or even around your house and attic, and they are the perfect place to try your hand at designing a small but complete piece of art. If your floors and walls are already covered with your work—and you are at the point where you even have rugs rolled up and stored away—here is a freestanding solution! They also make greatly appreciated gifts.

The Square Mixed Media Log Cabin rests on top of a footstool finished in Naugahyde.

    There is a way to "cheat" and merely place mats that look good atop footstools! I loved the way my *Square Mixed Media Log Cabin* mat looked atop a footstool that had been finished with black Naugahyde. I hooked the mat first, before I found the footstool. The footstool I found was the perfect size, but the Naugahyde on the sides of the footstool would have been ruined if I had tried to take off just the top and replace it with the mat. My solution was to just leave the rug resting on top of the footstool.

Bowls

Music Braid Bowl, 8½" x 6½"; **Hooking Braid Bowl,** 10" x 14"; **Branch Braid Bowl,** 10½". Various cuts of wool, silk, and taffeta on linen; traditional rug hooking, braiding, and knots. Designed, hooked, and braided by Kris McDermet, Dummerston, Vermont, 2014. KRIS MCDERMET

Kris McDermet recently combined braiding and hooking to make a series of wonderful bowls. Her goal was to make them colorful, functional, and strong, but also attractive and fun.

Lizard in A Basket, 5½" x 10" oval, wool on linen; traditional rug hooking and sculpting. Designed and hooked by Gail Dufresne, Lambertville, New Jersey, 2003.

Here is a wicker basket that I own (I did not make it!) that I made a little mat for. The lizard is sculpted.

118 | Rug Hooking with Fancy Fibers

Stuffed Creations

Some years ago, I became fascinated with making three-dimensional stuffed animals. My first stuffed three-dimensional piece was Jasmine.

Jasmine on Her Grassy Knoll, 14" x 15" x 3", #8-cut wool on linen (Jasmine) and 11" x 11", #3-cut wool, various yarns, and antique wooden bobbins on linen (grassy knoll); traditional rug hooking. Designed and hooked by Gail Dufresne, Lambertville, New Jersey, 2008.

The part I find most interesting about this piece is the grassy knoll, which was hooked with all sorts of #3-cut wool. I also used lots of different yarns. I pulled the loops up high and hooked as messily as I could to get the look of an unmown grassy field. I hooked four flat areas so the sheep could stand up within the field. I used this same technique for each of the bases for my stuffed creations.

Away in a Manger, 4" x 5" x 2", #8-cut wool and various yarns on linen (sheep) and 6" x 7", #3-cut wool and various yarns on linen (snow); traditional rug hooking and prodding. Designed and hooked by Gail Dufresne, Lambertville, New Jersey, 2008.

So far I have made two little sheep standing in a manger atop a snow-covered mat, a loon swimming in the cold water of a Maine pond, and my version of a shark attack. The inspiration for the shark came from thinking about a shark lurking through the water. The little fish was an afterthought. The piece was first meant to be displayed with the shark chasing the fish, but it takes on a whole different meaning when their positions are switched around. The fish could be chasing the shark, or they could be at a stand off! I have visions of a camel in his own oasis and some version of myself. Someday.

Loon, 13" x 6" x 4", #8-cut wool and yarn on linen (loon) and 8" x 18", #3-cut wool and various yarn on linen (water); traditional rug hooking. Designed and hooked by Gail Dufresne, Lambertville, New Jersey, 2008.

Shark Attack, 20" x 6½" x 4", #8-cut wool, google eyes on linen (shark), 6½" x 3" x 2", various cuts of wool, yarn, and google eyes on linen (little fish), and 10" x 24", #3-cut wool and yarns (water); traditional rug hooking. Designed and hooked by Gail Dufresne, Lambertville, New Jersey, 2008.

Frank-N-Wine, 14" x 15" x 3", various cuts of wool, novelty fabrics, yarn, buttons, and wine bottle corks on linen; traditional rug hooking and sculpting. Designed by The Potted Pear, hooked by Gail Dufresne, Lambertville, New Jersey, 2012.

My newest stuffed creation is *Frank-N-Wine*. Frank is not my own design, but I loved him so much I had to hook him. I used sparkly wool for his face and sculpted his nose. Note the strategically placed wine bottle corks.

Two To End With...

Last but by no means least are two of my favorite pieces. I hooked *Smoke and Mirrors* years ago, and I still love its simple, classy look. The other is a recently completed version of one of my designs, *The Candy Store,* hooked by Carla Littlejohn, who told me that making this piece was the most fun she had ever had hooking. She said that "once I started, the piece took on a life of its own and just flowed. It was pure happiness! Texture, glitter, shine, glitz, color, and imagination! Everything that makes me happy!" If you have been inspired as Carla was by what you have seen and read, then you are ready to unleash your own creativity!

Smoke and Mirrors, 5" by 9", #8-cut wool, Ultrasuede, novelty yarns on linen; traditional rug hooking. Designed and hooked by Gail Dufresne, Lambertville, New Jersey, 2005.

Candy Store Too (detail), 30" x 22", various cuts on linen, novelty yarns, Spandex, ribbon, silk, leather, satin, velvet, and anything else that caught Carla's eye; traditional rug hooking and trapunto. Designed by Gail Dufresne, hooked by Carla Littlejohn, Garland, Texas, 2016. GAIL DUFRESNE

Resources

American Hooked and Sewn Rugs: Folk Art Underfoot
Joel and Kate Kopp
E.P. Dutton & Company, 1975
ISBN: 0-525-47405-6

American Sewn Rugs: Their History with Exceptional Examples
Jan Whitlock with Tracy Jamar
Jan Whitlock, 2012
ISBN: 978-1-4675-4866-3

Cloth, Paper, Scissors:
http://www.clothpaperscissors.com/

Fiber Art Now:
http://fiberartnow.net/

Combining Rug Hooking & Braiding: Basics, Borders, and Beyond
Kris McDermet, Christine Manges, Diane Tobias,
Schiffer Publishing, 2011
ISBN: 0-7643-2557-4

Textile Study Group Of New York:
http://www.tsgny.org/

Contemporary Hooked Rugs, Themes and Memories
Linda Coughlin
Schiffer Publishing, 2007
ISBN: 978-0-7643-3789-5

Finishing Hooked Rugs: Favorite Techniques from the Experts
Various authors
Stackpole Books, 2013
ISBN: 978-1-881982-99-9

Geometric Hooked Rugs: Color & Design
Gail Dufresne
Stackpole Books, 2010
ISBN: 978-1-881982-71-5

Prodded Hooking for a Three-Dimensional Effect
Gene Shepherd
Stackpole Books, 2008
ISBN: 978-1-881982-61-6

Traditional and Standing Wool Rugs
Diana Blake Gray
Rafter-four Designs, 2009
ISBN: 1-931-931426-31-7

Sculptured Rugs in Waldoboro Style
Jacqueline Hansen and Trudy Brown
Rug Hooking magazine, 2007
ISBN: 978-1881982579

Dorr Mill Store
www.dorrmillstore.com,
800-846-3677

Hooked Rug Museum of Nova Scotia
http://www.hookedrugmuseumnovascotia.org/
1-902-858-3060
E-mail: hookedrugmuseum@gmail.com

Honey Doo Cutter
http://www.honeydoocutter.com/
315-926-5816

Bliss and Fraser-500-1 cutters
http://www.fraserrugs.com
276-694-5824

Bolivar Cutter
http://www.bolivarcutter.com/
902-543-7762

Rigby Cutters
PO Box 158, Bridgton, ME 04009
207-647-5679

Bee Line-Townsend Cutters
http://beelinearttools.com/
866-218-1590

Rug Hooking magazine
"Teacher Feature: Maggie McLea," Judy Fresk, September/October 2001

Rug Hooking magazine
"Cutter Class," Gail Dufresne, September/October 2004

Rug Hooking magazine
"Collaborative Response Rugs," Linda Rae Coughlin, June/July/August 2011

Rug Hooking magazine
"The Waldoboro Museum Rug," Jacqueline Hansen, June/July/August 2012

Dharma Trading company
http://www.dharmatrading.com/

W. Cushing & Company
http://www.wcushing.com/

Mood Designer Fabrics
http://www.moodfabrics.com/

Surface Design Association
http://www.surfacedesign.org/